# Take Your Shirt Off and Cry

# Take Your Shirt Off and Cry

## A Memoir of Near-Fame Experiences

# Nancy Balbirer

BLOOMSBURY

New York   Berlin   London

10/09

Published by Bloomsbury USA, New York

All papers used by Bloomsbury USA are natural, recyclable products made from wood grown in well-managed forests. The manufacturing processes conform to the environmental regulations of the country of origin.

LIBRARY OF CONGRESS CATALOGING-IN-PUBLICATION DATA

Balbirer, Nancy.
Take your shirt off and cry : a memoir of near-fame experiences / Nancy Balbirer.—1st U.S. ed.
p. cm.
ISBN-13: 978-1-59691-478-0
ISBN-10: 1-59691-478-5
1. Balbirer, Nancy. 2. Actresses—United States—Biography. I. Title.

PN2287.B156A3 2009
792.02'8092—dc22
[B]
2008045397

First U.S. Edition 2009

10 9 8 7 6 5 4 3 2 1

Typeset by Westchester Book Group
Printed in the United States of America by Quebecor World Fairfield

*For Joel*

# Contents

# Preface

**I once played** Helen of Troy in an egregiously bad production of *Troilus and Cressida*, and the *Village Voice*'s reviewer—who panned the show—singled me out, saying that the simulated blow job I performed in my one, tiny scene was incredibly "realistic." This wasn't just *any* tacky little pageant, you understand. It was *downtown*, yes, BUT—it was *Shakespeare*; I was *Helen-of-Fucking-Troy*, and *Phillip Seymour Hoffman* was in it, OK?

Seriously, though, I looked at it like this: everyone has to start somewhere. I know how it sounds, but I had taken great pains to analyze the feigned beej scene in the puristic manner of my former acting teacher, David Mamet. And in doing so, I chose to look at the character of Helen as a fabulous metaphor for the "prostitution of patriotism," emblematic of war's Pyrrhic victories: the more they all fought, the more ravaged and debauched their precious symbol became.

I knew it didn't matter that I was only onstage for about ten minutes in a play whose running time was a little over three and a half hours. I would be discussed at length, and thought about throughout. You don't just give make-believe head and then people forget you! I might be "abducted" up in my dressing room eating a cheeseburger, but I thought of this role as something akin to Meryl Streep's absent mother in *Kramer vs. Kramer:* out of sight but *never* out of mind. More important, I also told myself that playing Helen was a means to an end. That one day, soon after, I would progress to more meaty roles, playing women who, unlike Helen, had more substance (and stage time) than an incidental (let's face it) hooker. In fact, I saw myself perfectly cast as any of the Bard's principal feisty wenches, or the doomed dreamers of Clifford Odets, or even the jittery eccentrics of Tennessee Williams. I thought I'd play Stella in *A Streetcar Named Desire* in my younger years, then slip gracefully into playing the has-been (but still smokin' hot!) actress who beds the young hustler wannabe in *Sweet Bird of Youth.*

It was not to be. Helen of Troy was the sole Shakespearean character I played in my professional career as an actor; I never played in Odets; alas, I never played Williams, either.

And one day, I would come to see that there would be no trading up; my life in show business would be marred by near-constant head-banging frustration, demoralizing options, and bewildering compromises—and I'm talking about when I *was* working. In essence, I would come to view my acting career as nothing more than a series of fake blow jobs.

I had wanted to be an actor nearly my entire life. Some performers get their start through a desire to cheer up a miserable family member, and for me, that person was my mother. I can remember being a child of about nine or ten, impersonating Joan Crawford, whose movies I'd seen on the late show, to make my mother forget she was a bored, mostly pissed-off housewife whose fancy Upper East Side girls' school education had gone by the wayside.

One evening—the contents of our family dinner having erupted from the Crock-Pot an hour or so before—my mother stood stooped over the sink in a foul mood, scrubbing a pan, snapping at me, as usual, to bring her the dirty dinner plates. Suddenly inspired, I began running around the table, frantically grabbing plates, knives, forks, and glasses, pretending to be Crawford in the movie *Mildred Pierce.*

*"And then I worked as a waitress,"* I said, all panty with a throaty-fake-movie-star accent. *"And I got good—I got so good, I opened up my OWN restaurant . . ."*

My mother laughed. She asked for an encore and naturally I obliged. It was no small feat to make my mother laugh; she was not even remotely an easy crowd. Detached and indifferent, with a predilection for Scotch, she mostly preferred only the company of herself. She could almost always be found avoiding her children and housewifery, curled up on the porch she for some reason called a "Florida room," reading racy paperback bestsellers, whose covers depicted either a tendril-tressed lass with a plunging décolleté or a headless, partially clad woman in the midst of pulling off her wedding ring. Trying to get a reaction out of my mother—a woman seemingly roused only by *The Dinah Shore Show* (and even then, we're talking about *maybe* a few wan chuckles)—was marvelous training. I certainly enjoyed making her laugh, which was intoxicating, but even more I relished her prolonged attention. In our kitchen, *Dinah Shore* was never turned off completely, but soon, I became so entertaining that Dinah's sound got turned down. *Way down.* And not long after that initial Crawford impersonation, with my mother's help, I started in earnest to pursue a Life in the Theater.

In seventh grade, I starred as the Artful Dodger in the middle school production of *Oliver!* My mother, who long ago had harbored her own actress fantasies, not only chose the role for me but taught me a Cockney accent and coached me for my audition, coming up with "gestures" for each line of the song, "Consider Yourself." Playing the Artful Dodger changed everything. I was no longer entertaining in the confines of a joyless, avocado-colored, paisley-wallpapered kitchen solely for the benefit of my somewhat tipsy mother—now I was doing it publicly and, what's more, receiving accolades!

For once in my life, I felt I was good at something. For once, I wasn't being chastised by my teachers at school for goofing off or not being smart, nor was I any longer exclusively the object of other kids' scorn for being an unpopular loudmouth—instead I was being given respect, even admiration. I made a name for myself, playing the leads in every school and community production up for grabs: Adele Astaire in a sweeping Gershwin revue; Lola in *Damn Yankees*; Dolly in *Hello, Dolly!* My mother was beyond thrilled. Even my father, usually leery of show business ("All actresses kill themselves . . . look at Marilyn Monroe!") got on board, boasting to all his lawyer associates and judges about his "talented, Broadway-bound daughter." It was to become so much more: five years after my portrayal of the Dodger, I left the incarcerations of my *Ice Storm*-y Connecticut town and fled to New York, to attend NYU's Tisch School of the Arts, where I grew to love anything and everything about the art of acting. I loved, for instance, being someone else, in costume, with a totally different life, imagining that life, wondering about it day and night, and then inhabiting it. I loved the work ethic of the theater and the camaraderie of the performers, being backstage and watching the action from the wings. All my years at NYU, I thrived. I fancied myself an Artist who would never allow herself to be commoditized, perfectly oblivious to the fact that the people populating the world I would soon be entering were mostly interested in money and tits.

Perhaps in a sense I felt that I *deserved* success. After all, I had studied theater for many years, I had always received my mentors' support and encouragement, and more than a few of my peers had gone on to enjoy not just regular acting work but wildly flourishing careers. But if even a tad of entitlement was in evidence, it was almost always mitigated by unrelenting ambivalence. And that was the rub. Because as much as I could get off on playing the victim, flinging blame like strands of spaghetti at the wall, at some point I had to face my own complicity.

For many years, I existed in a state of near-constant terror that I would "not make it" as an actor. It was an awful, all-consuming fear, and I knew that if such a tragedy befell me, it would surely be so catastrophic, such a calamity, that I would never recover and the world would just immediately end. But when it happened, I stood, eyes tightly shut, steeling myself for the inevitable sky-falling moment, and when I finally opened my eyes, I realized that nothing had happened at all. Or it *had*, but it just wasn't what I had expected, and here is the most amazing thing: the impasse itself had become the opportunity.

I was a big flop—yes—all my dreams of being a working actor up in smoke, but my regrets, if I had any, were very few. And look: this won't be some pathetically sad rant about how unfair it all is—life, show business, the various inequities due to being of the tit-having persuasion . . . No. The phrase "Take your shirt off and cry" may appear at first a mere shameful indictment, and it was—once. But in fact, it was a remark a very wise person made to me in passing, one that I never forgot, as the years transformed it into an ebullient howl. And the best part? Nothing fake about it . . .

# Take Your Shirt Off and Cry

# 1. Take Your Shirt Off and Cry

**It is the fall** of 1983. I am a freshman drama school student at NYU, sitting rapt with attention as David Mamet, the guest lecturer in our seminar class, Intro to New York Theatre, expounds on why George Bernard Shaw had his head up his ass. I am a precocious seventeen-year-old clad in black leggings, glittery leg warmers, and white pumps. My gray sweatshirt has been expertly cut into a *Flashdance* neckline, and my eyes, rimmed and smeared with black kohl eyeliner, are wide open.

"Shaw told us that the theater is a teaching tool: people come see a play, learn what they're doing wrong in their lives, and then, go change," Mamet announces, deadpan, shrugging slightly. I dig his shorn hair, close-cropped patriarchal beard, and mustache. His round eyeglasses reflect the stage lights, an effect that makes him look like a Talmudic raccoon.

"That," Mamet continues, "strikes me as rather jejune, eh? It is *reductive* and it is *pretentious*. The *real* purpose of theater is to show the folks a good time—wow 'em—then, send them the fuck home."

Everyone around me is scribbling piously, but all I can do is smile. This guy is hilarious.

"Feelings don't matter, and neither do words," Mamet declares, stalking about the stage during the question-and-answer portion. He is admonishing a mousy freshman from the Strasberg Studio who has tripped onto a tricky philosophical land mine.

"The words are gibberish," he continues. "They mean nothing, feelings mean nothing. The only thing that matters are actions. It's only about *what you do*."

"But—how—how can you say that?" Mousy Method Chick sputters. "I mean, you're a playwright, of course feelings mat—"

"Excuse me—please, tell us, madam: how do *you* know what the character is feeling?"

"Because you—well . . . when you read—"

"HOW DO YOU KNOW WHAT THE CHARACTER IS FEELING? HOW?" he roars. "HOW DO YOU *MAKE* YOURSELF *FEEL*?"

"Well," Mousy Method Chick's face assumes the glow of raw hamburger meat, "you can d-d-do a 'sense memory,' like—"

"OHHHH!" Mamet puts his hands up, as if he's being robbed. "OK, thank you. [*Long pause*]. Folks, this woman—what she is referring to is JERKING OFF IN PUBLIC. She is talking about *Strasberg*. What Strasberg taught was to JERK OFF IN PUBLIC AND CALL IT ACTING. OK. Thank you."

Mousy Method Chick crumples into her seat in a daze as people continue to scribble:

*Feelings don't matter.*

*Do* not *jerk off in public.*

*Strasberg=Douche.*

"It's not your job to masturbate onstage," Mamet barks at us, his face impassive. "It's not your job *to be interesting*. Your job is to put your attention on the other actor in the scene, say your lines, and then," he adds merrily, "you go home."

Home. My mind wanders briefly back to Connecticut. I see

myself standing beside my father on the platform at the West-port train station, just a few weeks ago. I am leaving, heading off for school registration and my new life. My mother, whose enjoyment of cheesy melodrama is limited to fictional settings, has opted to stay home. My father holds my bag as I peer down the track, watching the ten thirty-seven pull into the station. I glance at him; he is shaking his head. "Don't worry, Nance," he says, smiling sheepishly. "It'll be OK." We hug, and I know that his assurance is more for himself than it is for me. "You can al-ways come home to your daddy, you know." His Brooklyn ac-cent seems especially thick when he says the word "daddy." *Dee-ahh-dee.* Three drawn-out syllables, as though the longer the word is, the more attached we'll be. The lush late-summer leaves wave a listless good-bye as I pull away and turn toward the open train doors.

"And don't *fah-get* what I told you: only take cabs! Don't *ev-uh* go into that shithole subway!"

Before the end of the lecture, someone asks Mamet who his favorite actresses are.

"Women who *act* are not *actresses.* They're ACTORS. Why do they need to fucking *qualify* what their genitalia are?" The audience titters; Mamet continues to thunder. "Folks, seriously, I need to disabuse you of the notion that 'actress' is anything other than a euphemism for 'floozy.' Do women doctors call themselves '*doctresses*'? [*Pause.*] Do women fucking writers call themselves '*writressess*'? [*Pause.*] NO! So why the fuck shouldn't a woman who *acts* call herself an *actor*?"

The lecture is over. Everyone laughs as we file out, and I am a new person: I will never allow anyone to call me an "actress" again.

\* \* \*

At the time, David Mamet was the preeminent badass of the American theater. The following spring, he would receive the Pulitzer Prize for Drama for his play *Glengarry Glen Ross*. Everyone at school (and elsewhere) was nuts about him. While I thought his whole vibe was killer, I was annoyed by how the older kids tried to approximate the Mamet ethos, traipsing about with Stepfordish reverence, constantly assuming a pseudo-intellectual, combative mien. They ate fruit-juice-sweetened granola, smoked high-grade pot, and traded in their contact lenses for Mamet-inspired coke-bottle glasses. They spoke robotically, like Mamet characters, repeating questions and statements with a bizarre quasi stutter:

"That's right. That's [*pause*]. Yes. *That's exactly so*," they'd drone at the Cozy Soup and Burger Diner near school, while ordering coffee. "Yes—I want it *regular*. Milk and sugar. Excellent. [*Pause.*] Yes . . ."

It was nauseating watching the Mamet-ites run around glassy-eyed, reeking of patchouli, saying things like "Swell" when you asked how rehearsal was, or the party, or the laundry room. It was Harold Pinter meets Charles Manson. I assured myself I would *never* be one of Mamet's minions.

Apart from Mamet's heady introduction, the first few weeks at school were mind-blowing on other levels too. Suddenly, men were checking me out in a big way. Walking through Washington Square Park, I'd notice guys staring at me, or I'd pick up my mail and find notes in my box from this guy or that, asking if I wanted to have coffee or check out some music at the Village Gate. I was so unused to this kind of attention that initially I thought it was a mean joke someone was playing on me. All through high school, I was a tomboy; only two guys ever asked me out. But somehow, the moment I arrived at NYU, I became fuckable.

My sudden popularity, however, did nothing to assuage a

lifetime of self-doubt. In fact, my newfound desirability had the paradoxical effect of making me more needy and desperate. I slept with almost anyone who asked. There were a few whom I merely made out with, just for kicks, but I was rapidly getting a reputation as an easy lay. On the sluttiness spectrum, I suppose I wasn't that unusual; this was, after all, drama school, where people would routinely screw their scene partners mid-rehearsal, then decide they were bisexual by dinner. Walking through the Drama Department halls, you would find yourself in a maze of bodies: people making out, giving massages, bodies draped across each other, legs and arms intertwined all over the lumpy, moth-eaten couch next to the bulletin board. There was once an entire *Hamlet* cast who gave one another crabs.

I can recall countless evenings spent listening to the ubiquitous strains of Tina Turner's "What's Love Got to Do with It," rolling around on some random artsy dude's BO-infested East Village mattress, wondering, what, in fact, *did* love have to do with it? I'd habitually show up to study down the hall of my dorm with guys from my History of Dramatic Literature class wearing nothing but a tank top and bikini undies, and when they'd look at me, astonished by my shamelessness, I'd act like *they* were crazy. I was a whirling dervish: voraciously horny, out of control, and, at the same time, deeply conflicted about the sexual attention I seemed to court so breezily.

I found refuge from all this male attention in a blossoming friendship with my dorm roommate, Therese, a shy girl also in the Drama Department, with a quirky, sharp wit. Therese and I immediately bonded over our mutual love of movies, Woody Allen's in particular. We liked to trade off Woody's and Diane Keaton's lines:

She'd say, "He's a genius, Helen's a genius, Dennis is a genius. You know a lot of geniuses."

And I'd say, "You should meet some stupid people—you could learn something."

We'd collapse with laughter.

Then I'd say, "You don't need a male. Two mothers are just fine."

And she'd answer, flawlessly, "Really? Because I feel very few people survive one mother."

Therese and I also shared the fact that we had Jewish fathers and shiksa mothers and for kicks, we'd run around Tompkins Square Park singing "Half-Breed" while annoyed homeless people tried to sleep. One day, we performed the entire song for a junkie who was lying on a bench.

"What d'you think?" Therese asked him after we had finished. He reflected for a moment and then offered, "Cher sucks."

From then on, whenever we'd ask for each other's opinion, no matter the subject, the answer was always "Cher sucks."

My father liked Therese. He met her when, after taking a deposition, he showed up on a whim to take me out to lunch and invited her along.

"Now, Therese is a *brawd* who *eats*," he enthused the next day over the phone. "Which is good: people who eat are *trustworthy*."

Therese and I had a blast; there was such ease to our connection, and a humorous rapport that continued to deepen and grow. As we got closer, our natural tendency toward joking about everything fell away, and through tearful, late-night analytical conversations, we were mutually able to arrive at epiphanies about ourselves, most of which had to do with having distant mothers from whom we craved warmth and tenderness.

We hugged, habitually brushed hair out of each other's faces, curled up together on one of our beds to listen to Joni Mitchell's

*Blue*, or Kate Bush's *The Kick Inside*, or the sound track to *Pippin*, crying, laughing, singing along softly.

I'd never had anyone be that affectionate with me without sex involved. Here, for the first time, was a person whom I trusted completely, who loved me just for me, not to use me or fuck me or get anything other than just my loving back. I felt safe with Therese; with her, I could let it all hang out.

"Why do you think that guy asked me out? You think maybe it's some fucked-up joke?" I'd ask virtually twice a week, standing in front of our chipped closet-door mirror, tying and retying the floppy rag bow in my hair, turning this way and that to get every possible view of the ass I thought was so fat.

"Because you're beautiful," she'd say patiently, lovingly, tilting her head to the side as she watched me from her desk.

I had become obsessed with my looks. I couldn't pass anything remotely reflective without double-taking, but as much as I wanted to be adored, I wanted also to be left alone; I wanted to be checked out, but in fact, I couldn't bear to be seen. Therese took all of my insolent contradictions in stride; she was calm and loving, and I couldn't remember anyone ever before being as tolerant of my foibles.


In the spring, Therese decided to see if she could get into the summer program David Mamet was holding in Vermont. She was miserable studying at her assigned studio, Stella Adler, and the thought of spending the summer with her mother in their cheerless colonial home freaked her out, so she pleaded with me to help her with the audition. Except that there wasn't an audition. Instead, Mamet asked that all applicants participate in a weeklong treasure hunt to uncover the answers to ten or so riddles. The answers were to be presented—typed up—to Mamet

during an interview, at the end of which the applicant would recite a memorized poem by Rudyard Kipling.

"You do realize that this is by far the most fucked-up thing
you've ever auditioned for, right?" I asked Therese one day
while we sat flipping through humongous reference books at
the New York Public Library.

She did, of course, but she was truly desperate. Therese hadn't
had any luck scoring roles in the school's classy Mainstage productions and had been relegated to trying out for the various
"experimental" student productions—usually plotless rumina-
tions on emotional breakdowns and scatological insights—that
left their audiences catatonic. She auditioned and auditioned,
but no matter how revolting the premise, she never even got a
callback.

As the year progressed, she grew increasingly depressed by
the rejections, downing cheap bottles of Bordeaux, then lying
in bed reading *Remembrance of Things Past* in the original
French.

So when it came time for the Mamet "audition," Therese
raced all over Manhattan and parts of Brooklyn and Queens
trying to unearth answers to the brainteasers, discovering that
most of them had to do with obscure World War II weaponry,
con-artist ploys, and arcane poker slang. At the end of the
week, with barely half of the correct answers, Therese wept un-
controllably as we ran through her Kipling poem.

"What do you think?" she whimpered. "Do I even have a
chance?"

"I think," I said, taking her hand, "that Cher sucks."

I sat next to her on the bed and wiped her tears with the back
of my sleeve.

The whole thing infuriated me. What kind of arrogant prick
was this guy, sending these hapless kids all over hell and gone

looking for cryptic crap? It was just a load of I-say-jump-now-you-say-how-high. What did any of this have to do with *acting*, which was what he claimed he'd be teaching them? Looking at Therese's puffy, red-blotched face as she sat blubbering on her squeaky dorm bed, clutching her hard-won typed-up answers, I thought back to that Mamet lecture.

"The only thing that matters are actions. It's only about what you do," he had said. "The words are gibberish; exercise your will . . ."

And then, the whole Mamet gambit dawned on me: Whatever the premise, whatever the score, it didn't matter. His thing was about showing up and committing wholeheartedly. It was, essentially, a game of five-card stud for stage.

"Therese, don't worry," I assured her. "None of this matters. All that matters is that you go in there and present this shit with pride."

"But," she wailed, "I'm missing a bunch of the answers!"

"Listen to me," I said, kneeling in front of her. "Just go in there, look him in the eye, and give him the answers you have— no apologies for the ones you don't—and do that poem like you mean it. Period. And tell him you *want* to study with him."

Therese was not only accepted; she became one of Mamet's most treasured students that summer. She sent me exhilarated letters detailing how he appreciated her "offbeat style, rapier wit, and deadpan delivery." He'd rave about what a great writer she was and he made her a founding member of the new theater company he started with all the kids who'd been studying with him the past few summers in Vermont.

When Therese came back to school in the fall, she was a new person. She had new standards for herself and would no longer audition for anything—Mainstage or not—without seeing a script first. Her posture, which had been schlumpy at best, was now erect, even graceful. People spoke about her when she walked into rooms: "Oh! There's that *funny* chick!" Therese was hot shit.

That semester was insanely busy for both of us. Therese was immersed with the new theater company; I was cast, much to my surprise and delight, in a few Mainstage shows. My favorite was my very first: Adrienne Kennedy's bold, surrealistic dream-play, *Funnyhouse of a Negro*, in which I played a blowsy, middle-aged landlady who spews hideously racist monologues directly at the audience as though performing stand-up. Costumed in a blonde wig, white kabuki-style makeup, and a fat suit designed by the Tony Award–winning Willa Kim (which took sixteen hours of fittings), I literally disappeared inside my role. Whenever I would meet people thereafter during my years at NYU, they would be astonished by this credit: "That was YOU in there??" It was a great source of pride.

My parents came to see me in *Funnyhouse*, and I found my father wandering around backstage after the curtain calls, dumbfounded.

"What the hell *was that*?" he wanted to know. "I *think* you were good, but I didn't *undah-stand* one goddamn word, so who knows?"

My mother and I tried to explain that the text was meant to be nonlinear; that it was lyrically brilliant, absurdist in the manner of Beckett . . . but my father wasn't buying it.

"Such a bore," he'd repeat, rolling his eyes. "You can't tell me people actually *like* this kinda crap. Why don't they do some Neil Simon, for Christ's sake? Now *there's* a genius . . ."

Despite my achievement with *Funnyhouse*, I began to get discouraged. I would get cast in parts and feel stressed out and insecure about my ability. I was constantly anxious and overwhelmed.

Watching Therese be so confident and inspired, I felt excited for her, but also a bit jealous. The change in her was so striking, I started romanticizing the Mamet experience. Maybe it was cultish, but it seemed to work for Therese. I wanted a piece of that too.

When Mamet announced the inception of a new year-round acting studio at NYU, to be held at the Vivian Beaumont Theatre at Lincoln Center for only fifteen new students, I put my name first on the list to try out. Students would be instructed by Mamet's protégés; Mamet would teach master classes a few times a month ("subject to availability"). I asked Therese, who would be moving on to the advanced "company classes," to coach me. Unlike the high-wire hat trick Therese had had to endure to get into his summer program, my interview was a run-of-the-mill audition, wherein I would perform a monologue for a Mamet protégé and the voice teacher. At the time, I was on a bender of feminist-inspired rancor against all the same old boring victimy-chick monologues, like those in *Getting Out* and *Crimes of the Heart*, plays I referred to as "Menstrual Shows." I insisted on only doing guy's monologues in class and for auditions. For the Mamet-studio audition, I chose Jerry's speech from Edward Albee's *Zoo Story*, known as "The Story of Jerry and the Dog."

"Just do what they tell you," Therese said as she threw out various outlandish ways for me to approach the text. "Don't worry about it *making sense*. Just, whatever objective they tell you to try, do the monologue that exact way, with total confidence and commitment."

The advice was strangely familiar.

"When they ask you what you'll do if you don't get in, tell 'em you'll quit school and go off to 'work on your voice.' They'll love that. And just remember," she smiled, throwing the Albee script at me, "Cher sucks . . ."

I had a great audition, and the following day I literally jumped up and down when I saw my name on the list posted on the Drama Department bulletin board. Therese and I decided to celebrate by going out to dinner at a French bistro called La Metairie, a teeny little jewel of a joint on the corner of West Tenth and West Fourth. The place had a rustic vibe, smacking of Provence, complete with beamed wooden ceilings artfully festooned with copper pots and farming tools. There were even doves—real doves cooing in cages—perched above the diners, tucked between baskets of hay and dried hydrangea. It was adorable; even the butter was adorable, fashioned in the shape of a duck.

"I love you," Therese said, after the waitress left our table.

"I love you too," I said, holding aloft the kir royale I'd felt so terribly sophisticated ordering. "To us!"

"No," she said, taking my hand. "I mean . . . I *love you* . . . "

"Oh" was all I could manage. Therese sat across from me, the candlelight dancing fretfully across her flushed cheeks.

She continued to hold my hand and stare at me, batting her eyes in that languid way cats do when they worship you.

I was both startled by her confession and somehow anticipating it. We always said "I love you" before getting off the phone, before going to bed at night, at the end of cards and letters. And I *did* love Therese, but—did I love her *like that*? I never felt like fooling around with her, though I did find myself at times rolling over the same familiar fantasy in my mind: "God—she's brilliant. I wish Therese was a boy."

"So . . . are you a lesbian?" I asked, wishing we could go back to the halcyon days. It was clear we were entering a new era, fraught with doom.

"No," she shook her head, bemused. "I'm just in love with *you*."

I nodded, trying to grasp the distinction. The butter duck was melting. Most of the bottom of it had liquefied, so that it appeared to be just the head and part of a wing, swimming in its own excrement.

"And," Therese continued, "I want to kiss you."

"OK," I said. "Here?"

"No, no, that would be . . . weird, I think—don't you?"

"Yeah," I said, subdued, examining the butter dish.

After dinner, we took a cab to Queens, where Therese's parents owned a vacant apartment in Forest Hills. There, we lay on the beige wall-to-wall carpeting of an unfurnished postwar condo, and to the yelping strains of Spandau Ballet's *True*, we made out for several hours. I wanted to be turned on, but I wasn't. For the next few months, I would make out with Therese one day and for the next two weeks pretend it had never happened. I thought I could make the fact that I wasn't gay go away if I just didn't think about it. It was a very Scarlett O'Hara "I'll think about it in the mornin' " type of denial. I just didn't want Therese to be mad at me—couldn't bear it, in fact—but that's, of course, exactly what happened.

"I always knew you were a cock-tease, but it looks like you're a twat-tease as well!" she railed one morning after I'd brought home a guy I'd picked up at a Freeing the Voice seminar the night before.

I was whirling back and forth emotionally, either berating myself for my perceived sluttiness or feeling defiant in my unbridled pleasure-seeking. I needed her to love me; I needed things to be the same. Together, we had become successful. We had given each other the space and the love to be better; what would happen if it all came crashing down?

\*   \*   \*

For our first class, David Mamet delivered a lecture the premise of which was that Bill Cosby was a whore. This was certainly a cutting-edge way of viewing him, given the popularity at the time of *The Cosby Show*, and we all sat in our seats, completely riveted, furiously writing notes into our notebooks. Cosby was a whore, television was evil and for whores, Hollywood was a hotbed of whoredom, and we were to avoid all of these things like the plague, unless, of course, we too were whores and not the artists we'd said we were. Why it never occurred to any of us to question the fact that Mamet himself was actively working in Hollywood, toiling away on movie scripts and, furthermore, television, is beyond me. Maybe we intuitively understood that he wanted us to be "pure" in some parental way, a sort of don't-do-what-I-do-do-what-I-say. It reminded me of my father, sitting in his underwear at the dinner table chain-smoking Marlboros and berating me for smoking.

"It's vile," he'd sneer, blowing smoke in my face. "I just don't understand it. *How can you smoke?* You're gonna ruin your singing voice after I paid for all those goddamn lessons!"

If these subtle ironies eluded us, perhaps it was just our sheer excitement. Mamet was forever blowing our minds with his contrarian edicts, like the time he told us that for an actor there was "no such thing as character." Character, he declared, was the job of the playwright. No matter how vigorously we argued our position that actors had a huge part in the creation of their roles, Mamet stood impervious, arms folded, having none of it. It was infuriating. But it was also a total turn-on.

Often, Mamet would begin his sessions with us by reading aloud an incendiary essay he'd written the previous night, embracing themes near and dear to his heart. Banalities on Broadway was one; critics, whom he referred to as "the Syphilis and Gonorrhea of the Theatre," were another. Mamet rained down his most vigorous contempt, however, on Hollywood film producers, who he insisted were nothing more than a bunch of self-loathing Jews obsessed with making bad films about nice Nazis. His style was rather breathtaking: each essay was a rhetorical rant, artfully interspersed with potty-mouthed hyperbole, after which he'd take questions (if you dared), and he always presented each of us with our own essay copy to take home as a parting gift. Turtle Wax, Mamet style.

As fun and entertaining as Mamet could be, he was a dogmatic hard-ass about rules and respect for theater as an art, and woe to the person who challenged him. We were instructed from the outset that if we did not show up to class fifteen minutes early, we would be considered late and not permitted inside. No exceptions. No excuses.

"There are no accidents. People do what they want," he told us after throwing out a guy who came in at five of with a whole story about being trapped in the subway for an hour. Mamet's intolerance for lateness was extreme, as was his reaction if someone was doing an exercise or a scene and he couldn't hear them.

"GET THE FUCK OFF THE STAGE. NOW," he'd bellow from the back of the darkened Beaumont. "And," he'd continue, his short, burly body bouncing around like a schoolyard bully in need of his daily Ritalin, "don't fucking come back until we can hear you. *How dare you*? You're WHISPERING. On the stage. It's fucking passive-aggressive!"

As the disgraced culprit would slink off the stage and back to their seat, Mamet would press on.

"You know, folks, only people who are full of shit *whisper*. It's a fact. They *whisper* because they are fucking *liars*. Once again: your job is to tell the truth. People think that to be a good actor you must be a good liar. No. A good actor is good at *telling the truth.* If you are not full of shit, if you are not *lying*, you speak *so people can hear you.* It's that simple."

I thought he was so terribly hip, mixing cocky, intellectual expressions like "This is exactly so" and "edification" with Yiddishisms and raunchy jokes.

The tension in the air during his classes was palpable, and everyone always seemed meek and nervous about volunteering for exercises, but somehow, the more bellicose Mamet got, the calmer I felt. His two-fisted style may have freaked out my classmates, but I felt right at home: he reminded me of my father, aphorisms and all. It was like déjà Jew.

"You get nowhere being afraid of me. Nowhere," Mamet declared one afternoon, looking around the room with dismay. "Who wants to try the prologue from *Henry V*?"

My hand shot straight up.

"Me. I do!"

"OK. Good," he said, handing me the book. "I want you to do it like you're 'imploring a loved one to give you another chance.'"

"O for a muse of fire that would ascend the brightest" was all I got out before Mamet blurted to the class, "OK, this is very good. *She's* not afraid. This is good."

"So, *nu*?" Mamet asked, turning his attention back to me. "Have any 'actions'?" "Action" was his term for what was commonly referred to in acting parlance as an "objective"—or the thing that you, as the character, want and thus are trying to achieve in the scene. Mamet had asked that we keep a running list of actions to have at our disposal, so that we could use them in our work and also discuss them in class.

"Yeah. I'm in rehearsal for a production of *The Maids* right now. I play Madame, and I think this is a good one to use on the maids: 'Get these assholes to cater to my every whim.'" Mamet's eyes widened, and he looked up to the ceiling.

"Well, OK . . ." he said, beginning to laugh as he considered it. "It's a bit over the top, but it works. And, it's funny."

"There's also a bunch of times where I use 'putting an asshole in her place,' but it's not as fun as the other one."

"So perhaps we need to investigate ways to make it more fun for Nancy to do," Mamet said, addressing the class. " 'Putting an asshole in her place' is the essential action," he said, turning his attention back to me. "It's 'as if,' what?"

(The "as if" was the last step in Mamet's technique. It was used to help the actor better understand and personalize the action they had chosen. Using your imagination and your own words, what does the action mean to you?)

"It's as if I could tell the English teacher I had freshman year to stop patronizing me."

"Excellent—go."

"*Look, asshole, I'm gonna tell you this for the last time: DON'T CALL ME HONEY. OK? My name is not 'Honey.' You wanna tell me something, you wanna address me, USE MY NAME. It's Nancy. N-A-N-C-Y. Get it? NANCY! Like the First Lady. Only, actually, nothing like the First Lady, except maybe for the part where I 'Just Say No' to assholes who insist on calling me Honey, despite the countless times I have asked— nicely—to be called my name, which, in case you've forgotten, is NANCY. Oh, and by the way? I totally know that you thought I was a moron because I didn't know what the fuck a gerund was, but guess what? I have finally figured it out! Here, I'll use one in a sentence: 'Excuse me, but do you mind my ASKING YOU TO GO FUCK YOURSELF?'*"

"OK, this is exactly so," Mamet said, cutting in. "We have found an 'as if' for the action 'putting an asshole in his place.' It was simple, it was clear, and it looked fun. Was it fun?" He asked me.

"Very."

"Good. By the way—do you write?"

"No."

"Well, you should. Write a one-act, maybe. Why not?"

"Hey, Nance, how's it feel being the teacher's pet?" asked Charlie, one of the guys in my class, during a cigarette break.

"Aw . . . shut up. Don't be a douche," I said, firing up a Camel.

"You know he just wants to fuck you, right?" he asked, grinning a nasty, malevolent grin.

"Fuck *you*. He thinks I'm *good*. That so hard for you to believe?"

"I'm sure he does," he laughed, pinching my ass. "Good at *what*, though?"

"Be sure not to choke to death on all those sour grapes you're sucking on. Dick."

I didn't want to entertain the thought that even a whiff of what Charlie was saying was true.

"Come on, Nance," he said, giving me a wink and bumming a drag off of my cig. "Don't be pissed. You're a total piece of ass. No shame in that!"

There was, in fact, plenty of shame in that. I needed to believe that if I was a "teacher's pet"—in Mamet's class or anyone else's—it was because they thought I was good, not because they found me attractive. I didn't dare imagine that it was possible to be both.

"You can act with the Boys," Mamet commented one day after I did a portion of his "Fucking Ruthie" monologue from *American Buffalo*. "Good for you."

The monologue, as well as the play, is written for men, but I was hot to work on it. It's about betrayal of friendship in the name of "business" and what happens when someone's ethics clash with their desire to succeed. But it's also about the corrosiveness of anger and how, in the end, people betray themselves. I had an innate sense about these themes; I felt I understood them.

"He's very cool," I told my father when he picked me up from the train station for Thanksgiving. "He's, you know, real smart and he's this great writer. You'd love him: he's from Chicago and he smokes a cigar . . ."

"Is he a *faygele*?"

"No! How do you come up with that?" I said, laughing and incredulous. "What of what I just told you makes you think he's gay?"

"I dunno, he sounds like an asshole," my father said, yawning. "You know what they say about guys who smoke cigars, dontcha?"

"No . . ."

"Small dick." He looked at me. "It's true."

"And you know this how? You've conducted a study? I mean, Jesus!"

"Common knowledge."

"Whatever. Anyway, he's great, really nice. He just started a theater company with all the kids, you know, like Therese, who studied with him up in Vermont—"

"How is Therese? She still fat?"

"She's fine. Anyway, so David Mamet bought all the kids in this theatre company jackets. You know, company jackets that are really cool. He even got their names sewn on."

"So what? Small price to pay to feed his no-doubt-huge ego, you ask me."

"You always hate everybody . . ."

"What're you *taw-king* about?"

"Everyone I like: Barbra Streisand—"

"*Oy vey*—"

"You hate her."

"Barbra Streisand is a *dawg*."

"She is not!"

"An absolute beast!"

My father and Barbra had grown up together in Brooklyn. He wasn't exactly a fan.

"No, you have some kind of weird thing against her . . . something about growing up in Flatbush and shared misery, and—"

"My only misery is when I have to fucking *look* at her. Christ, what a *meeskite*."

"You're so limited. According to you, there is only one way to be beautiful, and it's blond, with big tits and a small nose. It's sexist, and it's self-loathing, and it's, you know . . . totally anti-Semitic."

"Oh yeah? You think you're *so smart*, well, lemme tell YOU something, Nancy: You're getting to sound awfully *shrill* and *strident*, like one of those *big-mouth brawds*, AND I DON'T LIKE IT. You wanna start in with this kinda crap, I'll put you on the train, send you right back to the Village, and you can have Thanksgiving with fucking Gloria Steinem!"


After Thanksgiving, things with Therese really began to deteriorate. She had started taking classes in experimental theater, and somehow even her advances were assuming an avant-garde flavor. After staying out till all hours, knocking back pitchers of sangria at Panchito's Mexican restaurant on MacDougal Street,

Therese would arrive home, crawl into bed with me, and recite Aristotle's *Poetics* to the tune of "Back on the Chain Gang" while cupping my breasts.

"This has to stop. I can't take it—I can't do this anymore!" I yelled one night as I pushed her away and stormed out of bed. I flipped on the light. Therese sat, clutching my pillow like a baby and weeping.

"I knew you were falling out of love with me," she moaned. "But you didn't have to rub my nose in shit by fucking that . . . that . . . *homunculus* while I'm lying in the other bed!"

I had recently begun sleeping with a guy from the Film Department. He was very short.

"Look . . . I don't know what to tell you. I'm not in love with you! I-I've never been *in love with you*. I *love* you, just . . . not in that . . . not like, you know . . ."

"FUCK YOU," she exploded, throwing the pillow at me. "You fucking *stomped* on my heart. You fucking just ripped open my chest, pulled out my heart, and fucking just . . . annihilated me!"

"Therese, please . . . you know how much I care about you, but this is just . . . you know what I mean, I just . . ."

"HOW?" she screamed, throwing herself on the floor. "How can you do this?"

"Do what? What have I done? I'm just telling you my feelings," I said, sinking down next to her.

As horrible as I felt about hurting her, I couldn't help also feeling angry about being in this situation and about Therese not just being cool and "getting it." But I was nineteen years old, far from savvy about the intricacies of expressing myself. I'd known what I needed to tell her ages before it came to this crazy scene, but I hadn't had the wherewithal or the wisdom to speak up.

Therese ran to the bathroom and locked the door. We didn't have pills, but we did have disposable Lady Bic Razors, so I followed her.

"If you don't open up, I'll get the RA," I said, banging on the door. When she finally emerged, she walked past me, in a sort of catatonic stupor, and started packing her things.

"Where are you going?" I kept asking her, but she just mutely continued folding and stuffing. She was done with talking. When she finished packing, she zipped up her bags and duffle and looked up, briefly, into space, as though she saw someone there, and she smiled, wiping away her stream of tears. She stood for a few minutes, crying and nodding at whatever it was she was looking at, like Jennifer Jones seeing the vision of the Virgin Mary in *The Song of Bernadette.*

On her way out, she told me that someone, someday, would break my heart into a million pieces, just as I had done to her. She was right, of course; someone did, and when it happened, I wondered, in the way that one does in desperate moments, if my Therese fiasco had completely screwed up my good standing in the Universe.

I was heartbroken and terribly ashamed, and since I had never confided to anyone what was really going on between Therese and me, I had no one to talk to. About a week after she left, I was wandering around the East Village when I ran into my friend Dennis, a wonderful, kooky intellectual with a penchant for William Burroughs. He invited me over for a cup of coffee at his book-strewn railroad flat on Fifth Street, where, in the dim, lava-lamp glow, I spilled my guts. I told him about the Therese make-out sessions and how it had just all gotten out of hand and that I felt like an awful person for leading her on. I also told him that I was scared of the Universe being mad at me.

"You think the Universe gives a flying fuck about that?" Dennis said, firing up a Marlboro Light and exhaling through his nose. "Come on! You're not a Nazi! You're not, you know, fistfucking retarded children. You didn't wanna *munch rug*—so be it! Trust me, the Universe really doesn't care about stuff like that . . ."

As good as it felt to unburden myself about the whole debacle, I was still miserable. I had lost my best friend.

Mamet's appearances in class, never regular to begin with, seemed to dwindle as time wore on. Though we were told that it was work that kept him away, I suspected that his complicated relationship with academic institutions contributed—at least in part—to his prolonged absences. When he did grace us with his presence, there was always a great deal of pomp and excitement. And he never disappointed: always with big stories about small men; funny, pithy observations; and a dirty joke or two, mixed seamlessly, as usual, into class exercises or scene work. After one of these classes, near the end of my last semester, I was walking through the bowels of Lincoln Center, toward the subway, when I stopped to light a cigarette.

"Got a light?" I heard a voice say. It was a question, but since there was no inflection, I turned as I lit. It was Mamet, holding an unlit cigar. I obliged his request, and we walked for a while, through the warren of dimly lit corridors, past empty rehearsal rooms and dressing rooms and costume and prop shops. I don't remember what we started out talking about—class that afternoon, probably—but whatever it was led to a brief conversation about actors, in general first and then, in particular, me. Walking through the Beaumont stage door and into the parking garage, we paused for a moment between the street and the mouth of the long tunnel that separated the theater complex from the number 1 train.

"You've worked hard. Good for you," he told me. "Good work; you're very good. I won't say you're talented. I don't believe in talent; talent is meaningless. The only thing that matters is your *will*. If you exercise your *will*. That's the only thing that means anything. And courage. You seem to have courage. Good. That's good, 'cause you'll need it."

He paused for a second, looking at me ruefully.

"There's nothing worse than being a woman in show business. Being a woman in this business, you'll be asked to do only two things in every fucking role you ever play: take your shirt off and cry. That's it. Take your shirt off and cry. Still, there's no reason that you can't do those things and do them with dignity and the scene properly analyzed. Be brave. Be strong. Are you writing?"

"No . . . not really. Not at all."

"Why not?"

"I just . . . I don't think I can."

"I know. Do it anyway. I know it's hard. Do it anyway. When something's hard, just do it anyway. That's all you can do."

Mamet told me he was going out of town for a few weeks, and when he came back, he expected me to have written a one-act, which I was to cast, direct, and present to the class.

"And if there's no play when I get back, I'll fucking fail you," he said, turning abruptly and walking toward the street.

"I thought you said you don't believe in grades."

"I don't," he said, and then he was gone.

I put off dealing with the one-act until the night before Mamet was due back in class. I freaked out, smoking and pacing around my dorm room, having no idea how to even start and, without Therese, no one to bounce ideas around with. I forced myself to sit down and at least stare at the blank page. In my mind, I could hear Mamet say, "Tell the truth . . ."

I contrived a single-scene play that aped the whole Mamet vibe with a role reversal involving a girl and a guy on a first date at an upscale coffee shop. I called it *ONE ACT* and followed Mamet's rule that there should be minimal stage directions. Other than placing the location, the only stage direction I gave was that as the guy spoke (floridly about "the meaning of Theatre and its cultural implications in the '80's"), the girl ashed her cig into her melted hot fudge sundae. The guy spoke without interruption for a few minutes, after which there was a long pause.

*The GIRL puts her cigarette out in the sundae and finally speaks.*

GIRL
So—do you want to fuck me, or what?
                (*Pause.*)

GUY
What?

GIRL
I said do you want to fuck me, or what?

GUY
I (pause)—I...I mean...well, becau—I...you
know there was a—

GIRL
Look, babe—let's just be real: we are here
now because you saw me at the *thing* and you

wanted to fuck me and I am here because I
thought, yes, that seems like it would be
excellent. That's what I thought. (*Pause.*)
Thinking empirically. (*Pause.*) When we met.
(*Pause.*) And, forgive me, I don't (and I'm
not being, I don't think, presumptuous in my
postulation), but I don't think we need to
waste all this time with niceties and all
that crap. Why all the talk? *We know what
this is.* Am I right?

                    GUY
Well—

                         (*Pause.*)

                    GIRL
Yes?

                    GUY
It's not only that—I mean, I think you are
lovely and I—

                    GIRL
What? I'm sorry—I can't hear you. Why the
fuck are you whispering? (*She leans in.*) You
know, only people who are full of shit
whisper, and I would hate to think you were
full of shit.

                    GUY
Well, I'm not. I'm—

                              GIRL
Yes?


                              GUY
I'm very, very—
                         (*Pause.*)


                              GIRL
What?


                              GUY
Sincere.


                              GIRL
Excellent. Then, what are we waiting for?


There was giggling from the moment the guy started his long-winded monologue, but when the girl uttered her first line, "So—do you want to fuck me, or what?," the room exploded with laughter and applause. I couldn't believe it; I had been getting laughs as an actor practically my whole life, but nothing ever compared to the sound in that room and the way I felt. I was extraordinarily moved. From across the room, Mamet nodded to me—a sort of touché nod—then stuck out his tongue and grinned. My eyes burned a bit from the tears that were brewing, and I sat in the back, listening to the laughter.

## 2. Ball and Chain

**One of my** first jobs out of school was playing a rotating succession of floozies—some dumb, some angry, all crazy—on MTV's first-ever nonmusical program, *Remote Control*. The parts were tiny, but *Remote Control*, the cultish late-eighties game show in which three college kids confined to EZ-Chairs answered trivia questions about television and pop culture, was a big deal. Often presented in mini-sketch format, the questions were posed by comics, who'd pop out in different characters when their "channel" was selected.

My friend Sam from NYU, already a semiregular, had suggested hiring me as a replacement for the sole female spot on the show, a Carol Merrill/Vanna White type who stands around looking foxy in Body Glove swimwear, mutely waving toward prizes. I knew I wasn't right for the job. I had way too big of a mouth to ever just stand around as set dressing, and though I looked OK in skimpwear, I wasn't exactly *Sports Illustrated* material. But Sam had come up with what the producers thought was a wonderfully novel idea: what if the Body Gloved Babe was *funny*; what if she could create and play characters, like the guys, thus making her more like, you know, a real person? "Great idea!" the producers cried gleefully, before telling Sam to have me show up for the audition in a bathing suit.

In the past, this might have set off alarm bells, but at this point, I was so excited I didn't care, and all the way over to the MTV offices, images of being the new Goldie Hawn go-go danced through my head. The audition itself was fun: I improvised shtick while reading commercial copy with one of the show's comic cohosts, after which I did a few of my impersonations: Debra Winger, Nancy from *Sid and Nancy*, and a lovesick Dino Flintstone. The fresh-faced producers, who were all very casually sitting on the floor sharing Chinese food, looked up when I was finished and with mouths full of dim sum said, "You're hired."

I jumped up and down when they told me, then ran around the room like an idiot ("YAY!!! WHEEEEEEEE! I LOVE YOU-UUUUUU!!"), throwing my arms around everyone.

"Hired on the spot," I whispered incredulously to my reflection in the darkened subway window all the way home. "What a great story!"

And it really would have been a great story, except that the next day, the producers had a change of heart, decided I wasn't "hot enough," and hired a model instead.

I didn't have an agent at the time, so Sam was dispatched to relay this news.

"They thought you were real cute," Sam told me, sympathetically. "They just wanted someone a little bustier, is all . . ."

To soften the blow, I suppose, they said they might, at some point, be interested in having me do some characters, though there were no guarantees, and it wouldn't be something regular. And that was it. Everyone had moved on, and some other girl was, at that very moment, being fit for all that glorious spandex.

But I took that bone they threw me and wouldn't let go. While I may not have cared all that much about the job before I auditioned—it wasn't exactly Shakespeare in the Park—the fact that they didn't want me because of my rack, or lack thereof, sent me into spasms of fury. This was to be my first "big" job out of school; I had spent the two prior years alternating between being completely sure I was about to be plucked from obscurity to become the next Julie Harris and thrashing about, bitter and angry that I was getting nowhere fast. All through my years of NYU—and even before—I was cast constantly. I never even considered that I wouldn't find work; I just knew I would. I was *that* confident. More than just having an enormous, pampered ego, I simply had no experience with rejection as far as acting was concerned. At least once during every show I was involved with at NYU, some theater professional or other would come up postperformance to praise me, flatter me, assure me that "if you want it, you can have it." Once when I was taking a curtain call, I heard someone screaming "Brava!," only to discover that it was my idol and total heartthrobbing crush, Mikhail Baryshnikov. Afterward, "Misha" came sweeping backstage to tell me, "Your eyes make me cry, but your hands make me laugh!" I didn't know what the hell he meant, but he was so hot I couldn't get over it. During those years, I felt the kind of invincibility that is truly only possible in the hermetic environs of art school, where we heard only about "The Work," and that "The Theater Is a Temple." To go from that rarefied place of exultation to the instantaneous struggles of not being able to get a job, or even an audition or an agent, was a crushing blow for my ill-prepared, puffed-up self. My whole identity was wrapped up in being an actor. It was something that I was good at and, at times, seemed like the only thing I could ever be good at, the only way I could feel worthwhile or lovable. What kind of cruel world wasn't *allowing* me to do it, I wondered over and over. What else could I even do? I had just spent my childhood, teenage, and college years devoted to one thing: being an actor. I wasn't trained for anything else.

"No luck, huh?" various *concerned* relatives would cluck over warmed-over deli platters at get-togethers, each event an extended exercise in abject humiliation, replete with unsolicited admonishing that I "find something to fall back on." Spacing out, I'd nod, listlessly staring into cheese spreads, whose gaping, stabby holes seemed to wink at my shame. I became violently depressed and took it out on anyone and everyone until I hated myself so much that I begged my father for money for therapy, something he vehemently didn't believe in (he always insisted that my depression was the result of not eating "three square meals a day").

Around this time, there was an audition for a movie, something I had fought hard to get, believing I was so right for the part that the powers that be could not help but cast me. All I needed was a chance to be seen. But after I read the scene, instead of saying "Great!" or "Thanks!" or "Meh . . . ," they said, "Turn around." They needed to see my ass. And as I followed this instruction, racking my brain to remember the part of the script where something about this character's ass was an essential plot point, I slowly turned my head around to see the casting director and his assistant exchanging glances. Unable to discern whether the glances were *good* or *bad*, I settled on *horrible*, and promptly stopped eating, at one point subsisting only on carrots until I actually started to turn orange. This certainly didn't help my moods or my mental state; it's awfully hard not to be pissed off all the time when you're starving. And I didn't want to go anywhere since there might be *food* and, well, that would be weird and too hard to be around. So, within a year of graduation, I was isolating and starving myself, alienating friends and family, and bickering endlessly and finally breaking up with my actor boyfriend, who, unlike me, never got cast in anything at school and, also unlike me, postgraduation got tons of auditions and jobs, even landing his admired ass on a gigantic jeans poster.

Then, as fate would have it, I met the Jazz Musician. I felt as though I had met my soul mate: another artist, a kindred spirit who understood. The ease with which I could share my sadness and confusion may not have quelled the turbulence raging inside of me, but for the first time, I felt heard, seen, and unconditionally loved. We were inseparable from our first date, when, as we walked hand in hand in the rain, he told me with awe that finding a great girl was even harder than finding a great drummer. He educated me in how to really listen to jazz, which I had always liked without paying much attention to why. Lying on his mattress in his teeny MacDougal Street bedroom, he'd fast-forward and rewind tape after tape on a junky boom box, explaining harmonics, interplay, stride piano, the beauty of broken phrases, how to identify the changes in the solos, and the clever "quotes" of tunes within tunes. I, in turn, fed his unquenchable appetite for any and all art by handing him a stack of plays from different eras—a mini-tour of dramatic literature—to devour during his near-constant travels around the world. He would call from far-flung airports and hotels in Rome, Sydney, Okinawa, or Miami, shouting into the phone, "Nance, this Aeschylus dude is one *bad* motherfucker!"

We chided each other about our respective love of crap: he'd kindly indulge my love of pop music by playing Neil Sedaka's "Laughter in the Rain" anytime we got near a piano, and to reciprocate this tender gesture, I would reenact scenes from the soap operas he watched while practicing his bowing in the afternoons. He was a brilliant talent, gifted, sensitive, and cool; he too had struggled, and now he was enjoying a regular paycheck, recording records, and hitting the big time. He got it. All my awful, angry feelings spilling out everywhere, all the crazy parts of a life in art that don't make any sense, all the feeling misunderstood, the jealousy, the unfairness—all of it, he got. I would sob to him over my frustrations as we lay on my apartment's parquet floor next to his bass, listening to Clifford Brown's *Yesterdays*, and he would rub my head with his giant, calloused hands and tell me to hang on, that my time would come.

"Everyone thought Monk was a retard till he was forty . . ." he would say gravely, and we lay there both comforted by this template and shuddering with the dread that "forty" conjures in the minds of those barely out of their teens.

So, when *Remote Control* came along, suddenly it became The. Most. Important. Job. Ever. I couldn't bear the idea that I'd had the gig and then, like sand, it had slipped through my fingers. I *had* to get on that show. For months, it occupied all my thoughts. I wrote the producers letters, called them up, tagged along with Sam on days he worked, whatever I could do to remind them of my existence. One day, about six months after the audition, I called up and told one of the writer's assistants that I was Glenn Close. When the writer (immediately!) picked up, I pretended to be Glenn as her Alex Forrest character in *Fatal Attraction*, demanding attention from Michael Douglas:

*"You don't expect me to be ignored—do you, Dan?"*

Well, it worked. He laughed, then invited me to the office to try out some character ideas I had (provided I left all cutting tools at home), and within a week I was on the show, playing

"Nancy," the game show host's Psycho Ex-Girlfriend from Hell. Costumed in a trench coat with rabbit ears sticking out of the pockets and clutching a large cleaver with which I gesticulated wildly, I made my entrance to the tune of "Love Is a Many Splendored Thing" whenever a contestant chose "the Ex Channel." After quizzing the contestant about their knowledge of celebrity divorces, I would beg the game show host, "Tell me you love me and I'll go," repeating this several times rapidly like a deranged mantra before being given the hook.

It's never great to be the Not Hot Girl on a mostly-male-audience comedy show. Still, I was insanely excited about the job, even if it wasn't regular and even if the parts were small. Invigorated by pride in my grit, relieved that I didn't have to be the flawless half-naked one, I was thrilled at the prospect of creating characters and being considered for my talent. I would be just like one of the guys.

The comics on the show were great to me; they were a hilarious group of guys, sweet and supportive, and I adored the babe they'd hired to be the Chick in the Body Glove Clothes.

All this initial rosiness wore off pretty quickly, however. For one thing, I was booed every time I made an entrance as the Psycho Ex-Girlfriend from Hell and could never shake how uncomfortable I felt, as much as I reminded myself that it was because I was "the villain." I wasn't used to being heckled; I wasn't a stand-up comic, and I would get flummoxed listening to the jeers. I would come backstage shaking and scared, the comics waiting in the wings, ready with advice.

"Don't let those douche bags throw you off your game. Ignore them!" I was counseled, but the reactions felt so hostile, so sinister, that it was impossible to brush them off. I also felt responsible for this monster to begin with, as though I had unwittingly put forth this grossly misogynist archetype, a fright fantasy, so abhorred by men that their only response could be to want to kill me.

"Don't overthink it," one of the comics told me when I recited this insight while we shared a smoke. "This shit ain't exactly Chekhov . . ."

I was always writing and bringing in new characters and sketches, but they were either rejected or revamped beyond recognition, while the guys' ideas and gags were rarely thrown out, and if they were, fits were had and lines or sketches immediately restored. Also, unlike the guys', my costumes got progressively skimpier each week, so much so that at times I was almost as naked as the Chick in the Body Glove Clothes, except usually with a ridiculous wig or bad hair, presumably to reflect my not-hot-ness. It didn't take long for me to figure out that instead of being in on the joke, I *was* the joke.

"Where are my costumes?" I cried to the cheery, disinterested producers. "What happened to my character?" I demanded of writers, makeup artists, cameramen, grips, craft services, and anyone else who would listen.

"Listen," one of the writers told me, "everyone *loved* your gag about being a punk rocker, but we've tweaked it a *little*, so that now you're the Rock and Roll Slut, a groupie who's fucked the entire music industry. You'll see, it'll be *awesome* . . ."

I wanted to feel awesome, I really did. But standing on the cold set in a bra with steel spikes, fishnets, and an Elvira wig, being mocked by frat boys, I felt stupid, ugly, and, worst of all, totally unfunny. The apogee of all this came when it was my turn to go out before the taping and "warm up the crowd" with cute jokes. I finally refused to do it after this exchange:

ME (*dressed as "Brooke Shields," with a scary* Valley of the

Dolls *sixties wig and cigarettes sticking out of my nostrils and ears*): "Hey, guys! Welcome to *Remote Control*!"

GROSS GUY IN SWEATS AND BACKWARD BASEBALL CAP, EATING COOL RANCH DORITOS: "Hey, where's the *babe*?"

ME: "Heh, well, you're looking at her! Isn't this a lovely getup? I got it—"

GROSS GUY ALONG WITH HIS GREASY-FACED, SIMILARLY UNIFORMED FRIENDS: "BABE, BABE, BABE, BABE, BAAAAAABE!"

Then they hurled the Cool Ranch Doritos at me until an usher threatened to eject them. Meanwhile, one of the other comics came out to save me from my death by Frito-Lay.

*Remote Control* was a very funny show with enormously talented people performing on it, writing it, and producing it, and I felt lucky to be on it, but miserable about the fact that none of that was because of me. I wanted to thrive there, but I didn't; the atmosphere made me feel unusually shy and intimidated and so far off from what I was naturally suited for that I bombed over and over. How I wished that I could feel supported or nurtured there, as I so resentfully surmised the boys were, but I also knew that as much as I pitched material, jokes, and ideas, I could never bring myself to go all out, to clear the unidentifiable hurdles that made me meek and listless.

"They're just being sexist," the Jazz Musician would always remind me, but I knew it wasn't that simple, and I refused to wallow in the familiar trope that it was my vag that made me a victim. I could see over the fence; I could see that what were required were brazen acts of will, refusals to listen to "no," and shrugs at the venomous shouts. I wasn't a killer; I wasn't aggressive like a comic, and I was used to being subtle—even coy—about my wants, needs, and desires when it came to my work and also my personal life. This, combined with my usual hesitations about what I really wanted, in the end snuffed out my enthusiasm.

Ultimately, I lasted only a season and what amounted to little more than a handful of performances on *Remote Control*; a season after that, the show was canceled. But before that happened, while I was still trying to get material on the air, be funny, and not have fun-size snack items tossed at my head, I woke up one morning to find the Jazz Musician crouched over the edge of the bed, sobbing into his hands.

"I can't do it, Nance. I'm sorry. I just can't be in a thing . . ."

I sat silently beside him, rubbing his back, my heart thumping as emphatically as one of his bass solos.

*You have to let me go*, he told me finally. *Of course*, I replied—how could I keep him beyond his will, even if I wanted to? But since this moment had arrived not after a fight or even a tense discussion, but rather, after a fun night out followed by extensive lovemaking and entwined slumber, I insisted he tell me *why*.

It was then that I learned that the person I knew best and loved more than anyone I had ever known—I didn't really know at all. He divulged various duplicities with groupies on the road, an old girlfriend, even some woman in New Jersey, with whom his only previous encounter, a year before we'd met, had been a quick screw on her futon followed by a sad little omelet heavily loaded with dill.

As the information tumbled out of his mouth, he packed up his belongings and pulled my cat from the curve in his bass where he lay sleeping. I could not speak, but inside I was screaming, "STOP HIM!!!!! DON'T LET HIM GOOOOOO!!!" He rolled his bass toward the door, the sun starting to rise and splatter across the parquet where we had lain each day and night listening to his heroes. All I could get out of my mouth, the only pathetic words that would come, were: "But . . . you *hate* dill . . ."

He nodded mournfully, then quietly slipped away.

What ensued for me was a near-suicidal breakdown the likes of which I had never experienced before—even amid despair over my acting career—and wouldn't again until three years later, when part two of our romance ended in an almost exact replay of this scene. For weeks, I wandered around my apartment and the surrounding blocks in a haze of self-pity, existential panic, and cigarette smoke. One blustery afternoon, I was trudging along Houston Street when I ran into Cary, an old director friend from school. I hadn't seen him in a while, and after a brief hug, I immediately launched into the one subject that occupied my mind: the blow-by-blow of my relationship's demise. Was it, I wondered aloud for the umpteenth time, due to my suffocating neediness, the Jazz Musician's incessant side-fuckery, or both? Cary, who was about to begin directing another of his experimental "pieces" about the nature of love and relationships, was positively enthralled. He insisted I join the cast.

"You're in a perfect place to do this kind of work," he enthused. "Lots of material to mine."

"I dunno," I groaned. "I'm sort of not able to be around actual people without crying or throwing up."

"Transmute it!" Cary cried. "Turn your throw-up into art!"

Now there was an appealing idea. Experimental theater had been all the rage while I was at NYU. There were always avant-garde luminaries passing through, creating new work with the students in classes and Mainstage productions. Some of it was brilliant, some of it shit, but it was always interesting.

When I ran into Cary, however, I was feeling rather dubious

about anything billed as performance art, having spent one too many evenings dragging myself up five rickety flights to bear witness to half-baked exercises in mental masturbation—the downside to any revolution. I rarely knew what the hell was going on in these "happenings" and spent most of the time watching other audience members willfully pretending to "get it," then smugly looking around in the dark to make sure other people had witnessed them "getting it," while the players strutted about the stage, conveying what could only be described as a telegraphed, finger-wagging "Fuck you." Eventually, all these performances blurred together in my mind, like an angry Mummenschanz skit, with lots of screechy music and always, *always*, dry ice.

But even if the prospect of being part of a team that created one of these things from scratch left me cold, I really liked Cary. He had a great sense of humor, which, along with intelligence and sweetness, he brought to all of his work, so I knew that whatever it was, it would at least be funny. Most of Cary's cast also happened to be friends of mine—either from NYU or from cater-waitering and cocktail waitressing—including my best friend, Bridget, so, there was that. I hadn't seen any of them in ages. I had dropped nearly everyone in my life in order to fully devote my energy to my relationship with the Jazz Musician, tagging along on the road with him at times, and when I wasn't doing that, I was trying to hustle auditions and working on *Remote Control*.

Standing on that windy stretch of Houston, dusk folding into night, cars whizzing by, I listened as Cary ticked off the details: the piece was to be part of some illustrious downtown theater festival in SoHo and something-something about Debbie Harry being involved. *Debbie Harry*. The hottest bottle blond ever, aside from Jean Harlow; the High Priestess of Cool; a woman unabashed about everything—her beauty, her glamour, her ambition—and whose every limp-lidded stare seemed to say, "Yeah. I'm fronting this band of boys, so put that in your pipe and smoke it." I worshipped and adored her. Suddenly, for the first time in months, I imagined myself having fun again: not being rudely heckled, but respected, admired, listened to with rapt attention, because this would be *thea-tah, dahling*! I knew, standing there in the dim light of day's end, that I would run, as I had done before and would continue to for many years, without a second thought back into the open embrace of that bitch goddess, Theater. Other jobs, men, friends, and family would come and go, continue to vex and disappoint, but fleeing to the squalor of some dark dump in a sketchy area of downtown would forever be my salvation, redeeming my folly, delivering me from the tedium of myself. The "Rapture" video flashed into my mind, only in this version, I was there too, kicking it with Blondie and the Man from Mars, eating Cadillacs, Lincolns too, Mercurys and Subarus.

"Count me in, Cary . . ."

Rehearsals for the piece, titled *Ball and Chain*, began the following week. We were given no script, only a conundrum: Why do we yearn for committed relationships, only to feel trapped when we're finally in them? Each rehearsal, Cary had us explore the paradoxical, often uneasy relationship of love and sex through a series of exercises and theater games, and he gave us take-home written assignments each night. The group, most of whom had worked with Cary on his other projects, consisted of five men and five women, including a hilarious girl from Queens named Donna, who, down to the accent, was a dead ringer for Cyndi Lauper. Twice a week, Donna had to miss rehearsals to tend to her very profitable business, Lauper-Grams, which involved, for a fee, showing up at someone's office party or birthday dressed as Cyndi and singing raunchy, made-up lyrics to the tunes "She-Bop" or "Girls Just Wanna Have Fun." The men were fairly standard overenunciating artsy types, goateed and gluten free. One of them, a chubby, coal-eyed Canadian, was so sensitive to women's plights and issues that he would often get choked up during our group meetings, or "energy circles," talking about the innumerable injustices we all endured because "ERA was never passed," or about how "beautiful" an experience it was to make love to his girlfriend under the stars near the Lincoln Memorial after the last pro-choice rally. He was very sweet, but that didn't stop me and Bridget from naming him Touch My Heart with Your Foot after Diane Keaton's weird actor boyfriend in *Annie Hall*.

We did all kinds of zany exercises at rehearsal to loosen up: We would write sex fantasies and give them out to another cast member to read aloud while still others acted it out in the background; we would walk around on "diagonals" until Cary shouted for us to freeze, whereupon we were directed to look into the eyes of whoever was closest to us and share a secret with that person, first only with our eyes, then later actually whispering into each other's ear. We would sit either in small groups or en masse discussing our breakups, fuckups, cheating and lying experiences, feuds, fancies, and best-sex/worst-sex-ever anecdotes. I was so utterly transformed by these experiences, I felt like Natalie Wood in *Bob & Carol & Ted & Alice* after she and Robert Culp come back from the Esalen Institute so "actualized" and wholly evolved that they can't wait to share their every single thought and feeling with not just each other but also their horrified best friends. I longed for rehearsal every day, desperate to be with them all again, honing what would end up as a series of mini-scenes of romantic circumstances and portions of relationships viewed at different stages of development. Although the piece wasn't linear, the individual scenes, clipping by at a lightning pace, suggested a single narrative about how we love and why, when it's something we all want, it's such a struggle.

*Ball and Chain* also aimed to explore power and gender and the ways in which the sexes feel empowered or not. During one conversation about strippers, Touch My Heart with Your Foot said that he felt bad for them, that surely they must feel nothing but shame and despair. This led to a sweeping discussion of breasts and how we felt about them as women and men, what they symbolized, what they stimulated, and why our culture was so weirdly obsessed with them. I myself had gone in circles about my own, never sure whether I loved them or hated them or should simply ignore that they were even there at all. Growing up, I felt at a disadvantage because they were small. Then, when I started having sex, I began to love and appreciate them because they gave me pleasure and because the men in my bed told me they were nice. My love affair with my own body came to an abrupt end when I started auditioning professionally and once again was at war with my body for being wrong and not enough. I saw how much power the Chick in the Body Glove Clothes wielded over the audience at *Remote*, the comics, the writers, and the producers, and I knew that my membership in the Itty Bitty Titty Committee kept me from being her. All the good-natured artsy dudes in the *Ball and Chain* company pooh-poohed the idea that men are, at their most essential, just look-ists who grow weak at the vision of boobage, sheep who are so visually dominated that they lose all ability to reason, etc., etc. Of course, they insisted that this was a sexist and retro way of viewing males; that they were not just "dirty dogs"; and that they were sophisticated and mature and had such profound re-spect for women and their bodies that, even though admittedly they thought we were luscious, they were beyond such horseshit.

"Let's see," I said, pulling my leotard down to my hips while everyone in the company's mouths flew open. I was just trying to be provocative, make them giggle with my smart-assedness. We laughed it off and moved on. But sitting in our group circle at the end of the day, we discussed how fun it would be to build such a moment into the show.

"It'd be a great 'objectification beat,' " Cary said animatedly. "In one pithy move, Nancy strides alone to stage center, surrounded by couples being couples, ritualistically tending to each other. She pulls out a cigarette, the top of her dress happens to fall, exposing her breasts, and all the men literally leap away from their inamoratas to flick her a Bic."

It was a manipulative stunt, silly, forced—this I knew—and yet oddly, I felt none of the recalcitrance that was part of my routine over at *Remote*, where I pouted and complained about skimpy costumes, whining that I was being taken advantage of as "a tool of The Patriarchy." Instead, I was intrigued by the cheekiness, and I suppose I wanted to know what it would feel like to be topless under all those lights, in front of a group of strangers and Debbie Harry. Besides, it was for a performance, and for free. Taking my shirt off for money—that would have been seamy. Doing it gratis, on the other hand, was an *artistic sacrifice*; I was like the Joan of Arc of the fringe theater scene.

"I feel like we're exploiting Nancy!" Touch My Heart with Your Foot exclaimed, sniffling, during the circle discussion after our final dress rehearsal, the night before we opened. I crawled across the circle to comfort him, caressing his head in my lap, while the others piled on into a group hug, like little lion cubs. As I shushed and reassured him and the rest of the company, saying that not only did I feel fortified by the topless moment but it was, in my mind, *essential to the piece's integrity*, I realized that, truthfully, rehearsing it, I felt nothing at all.

Then came the actual show. For all the numb nothingness of the times my top came down in our dingy rehearsal space, performing it live in the dark, bathed in hues of soft blue, was exhilarating. The faces of the first few rows, the only ones I could vaguely make out, bore startled expressions when first my breasts were thrust before them, but almost instantaneously, surprise morphed into warmth-tinged awe. I may not have been able to see beyond those first two or three rows, but the vibe in the space was unmistakably clear: we are here, together, beholding some naked tits, and it is all going to be OK.

I never once saw Debbie Harry during our brief run on Wooster Street, though our piece followed hers, but my mother was in the audience for our final performance. She had come alone in a hired car, then stood in line for an hour to get a ticket. I hadn't been expecting her; my father had sent his regrets, saying that he couldn't stay awake for a midnight show. ("What kind of show goes on so late?" he had asked. "They must be assuming no one will come, and far be it for me to prove them *wrawng.*") But my mother, ever the dutiful housewife, eternally submissive to the blustery protestations of my father, was not about to miss my return to the stage, with or without him, witching-hour moments of dishabille notwithstanding.

"What did you think?" I asked her afterward.

"I think your boobs are small," she said, cutting right to the chase. "But they look very pretty under the lights, and for that you should be damned glad."

I would go on to repeat the breast-baring act in subsequent performance pieces with Cary, and also for other helmers, becoming known in certain fringe theater circles downtown as the Chick Who's Willing to Show Her Tits in the Show If Need Be.

Though none of this shows were exactly like *Ball and Chain*, my toplessness in each of these outings was generally justified by the mini-themes that coursed throughout, usually having to do with contemptuousness for "the male gaze," positing the usual theories about "possession and ego," what it is to be an object both admired and deplored, and how when one looks at something, one sees not only the *thing* but one's *relationship* to the thing, blah, blah, blah. Whatever. All I know is that at some point in these melees, my shirt would come flying off. Show after show: bullshit, bullshit, bullshit, then shirt off, top down, bra off, show the groceries. And yet I loved it: the connection, the delicious albeit artificial intimacy I felt with the audience every single time. I couldn't help thinking that this was what one of the Method-acting teachers I'd had at NYU must have meant when she said that acting was the art of "behaving private in public." For many years, I convinced myself that I was being a brave feminist and a committed artist, that all of these pieces *really* needed such a moment. But I suspected—just a little—that these bits of nascent exhibitionism under the guise of "female empowerment" also served my compulsive need to make everyone happy, and I often wondered if all my supposed outrageousness made me any less compliant than usual. In any case, it got old and so did I, and several years later, in a theater in East L.A., I put my bra back on and stopped taking my shirt off—publicly, anyway. I was a little sorry to leave all that behind, wondering if I could ever again be that unadorned, that *naked*, but also, at the same time, that commanding of an entire room's attention? But feelings of wistfulness never lingered when I admitted to myself the truth: none of the times that had followed had surpassed that rapturous first with *Ball and Chain* when, ditched by my man, dissed at my job, I'd wanted nothing more than to act in the theater.

## 3. Mud Season in Maine

**Ned was the** best acting teacher I ever had. He made acting seem simple yet beautiful, no mumbo jumbo, nothing magical or elusive. There was an understated glamour about him like that of a rock star in the Eric Clapton or Stephen Stills tradition: not loud or rowdy, but "slowhand" and intense, occasionally dark, always witty. He also wasn't one of those creepy weirdos who seem to be playing out some psycho-Svengali fantasy wherein they "make you feel," like Ray, a teacher I had freshman year.

I remember once working on Blanche in that scene from *Streetcar* when her boyfriend Mitch says, "You're not clean enough to bring into the house with my mother." Right after my scene partner said that line, Ray punched me—hard—in the arm, and then, when I turned to him, horrified, he smacked me across the face.

"A breath went through you, yes?" Ray asked quietly, using his standard query line, his face a mask of placid madness.

Ned, being an actor himself, abhorred games like this and was both respectful and a straight shooter with his comments and critiques. Everyone—guys, girls—loved him and felt indomitable when he shone his approving light in their direction. "Yeah, I was hanging out with Ned," you'd hear someone gush, clearly feeling exalted by the proximity to cooler-than-shit Ned, Working Actor. An ex-hippie who, like most of the guys in his generation, played guitar serviceably, he was constantly throwing parties at his pad that would culminate in big Simon and Garfunkel sing-alongs. He was a voracious pot smoker, had eaten acid "like candy" through the sixties, and told intoxicating stories of marrying his first wife rather whimsically in a wheat field. He maintained that he'd never felt more "in tune" or "free" than when he was butt naked onstage in front of a full audience.

Ned cast me as the lead in a play he was directing that got me a lot of attention. I played a tough-talking, booze-swilling, pothead slut for whom the party could never end. The character presents herself as this freewheeling bon vivant, when in actuality she is a deeply insecure, mixed-up mess, terrified of being alone. It was a great part, and working with Ned was amazing; he made me feel safe. He got fantastic performances out of everyone in the cast and would take us all out to eat after rehearsals, his treat. Once, we were rehearsing this part where I made out with a guy in the middle of a chaotic party scene, and the guy—clearly taking advantage of the situation—started feeling me up. He was lying on top of me, being really rough; I couldn't move. Ned had a fit.

"Who the fuck do you think you are?" he yelled, throwing his clipboard on the floor and grabbing him. "Not in my show, motherfucker. Don't you dare take advantage of her or I will throw your ass right out!"

Because I had never been a partyer, Ned spent a great deal of time patiently teaching me how to roll joints like a pro (we used tea, which, because it smelled exactly like pot, caused quite the *scandale*) and how to mix cocktails with the unflinching poise of a seasoned drunk. The playwright—a well-known writer—was thrilled with the production and throughout the run would come backstage with her famous boyfriend and assorted fabulous luminaries, all of them breathlessly extolling my performance as well as Ned's inspired direction. A few nights after the play closed, Ned and I were hanging out and doing a little postshow recap. "You're gonna have one helluva career, Nance," he told me over a shared Caesar salad and fries. Later that night, when we stopped briefly at his apartment, he shoved his tongue in my mouth even though he had a girlfriend. I completely freaked, ran out of his apartment, and never wanted to speak to him again.

Seven years later, living once again with the Jazz Musician, I heard that Ned was in town and teaching a new class. Even though I was still disgusted by what had gone down between us, Ned remained the best acting teacher I'd ever had, and I was desperate to go back to class. I wasn't getting much in the way of acting work and was feeling very dejected about it. I couldn't believe that after all the promise I'd had at school, getting cast in this and that, I was washed up at twenty-seven. As Sandra Dee once said, I felt like a "has-been who never was."

I figured I was a grown-up woman now and the whole Ned debacle had taken place when I was just a girl. I told myself I had "moved on" from all of the resentment I had harbored in the months and years after the Pass. Besides, a part of me had always thought it had been my fault, anyway. I had probably been unconsciously flirty: "I led poor, hapless Ned on" is how that bit of reasoning would go. Never mind that when the Pass happened, I was twenty and Ned was thirty-five. Never mind that he was my teacher, someone I trusted, and also never mind that I had assumed he was faithful to his girlfriend, who had also been his student once and whom he had started seeing when his marriage had ended with a woman who had *also* been, yes, Ned's student. Ned liked to fuck his students—so what? I was the one with issues about it.

So, reminding myself of all of this, I signed up to be Ned's student again. And right from the get-go, it was great. Within weeks of studying with him, I started getting my confidence back, internalizing Ned's frequent morale boosts, feeling like, "Yeah, I'm actually good at this. I should be working."

"You've got a great voice," Ned enthused one day while we grabbed a cup of coffee and a bagel after class. We had fallen back into an easy friendship, picking up exactly where we had left off before the Pass.

"Seriously, you sound like Tammy Grimes. You could make tons of cash doing voice-over crap until you get a break."

"I dunno," I shrugged. "I can't even get in to see a decent commercial agent. I've actually done voice-overs before and kinda dig 'em, too. But I don't really have the money to make a voice-over tape, which apparently you need to—"

Ned waved this off. "I'll call my agent. You'll meet him and he'll send you out. You'll get some gigs; you'll make a tape from that. Done."

Sure enough, I went to see Ned's agent, who took me on right away, and soon I was making enough money to quit my terrible temp job. I started auditioning more often and landed a role in a short film starring Hume Cronyn. Things were looking up.

Then one day just before Christmas, the Jazz Musician announced that he was leaving me—again. "I am the reincarnation of Jack Kerouac," he told me. "I need to be free." Only two years before, I had taken him back, his previous indiscretions notwithstanding, because I hadn't been able to bear not being with him; otherwise, I'd thought, I would surely go mad. But then we moved in together, and I had gone mad anyway, raging at him for his duplicities whenever my insecurities got the better of me. I could never let it go. What we had shared in our relationship's first incarnation was gone—irrevocably shattered by both of us being who we were, while pretending to be who we were not. Somehow, despite our myriad problems, I had *still* convinced myself that we were getting married—a notion blighted, finally, by his past-life revelations.

Following his departure, I promptly forgot all about my career jump start and became morbidly obsessed with getting him back. I ate Xanax and called psychics at 900 numbers. I visited assorted tarot readers, whose readings I cross-referenced, scrutinizing them as though they were the Zapruder footage. I wandered, bleating pathetically, from one friend's apartment to the next, and when I'd exhausted those resources, I insinuated myself into the company of quasi acquaintances and strangers. I paced back and forth, clutching my sheaf of tarot readings, positing absurd questions and theories, while people sat tensely on their sofas, scared that whatever I had was catching. Eventually, no one would return my calls, and frankly, I couldn't blame them.

After I'd inexplicably missed a few of his classes, Ned got wind of my breakup from one of my scene partners. The next day, a basket from Balducci's arrived with food and cookies and coffee and a note that read, "I've been there, too. Thinking of you, your friend, Ned." It was such a sweet, kind gesture that all I could do was sink to the floor, shaking and mewling, clutching my goodie basket to my chest like a life preserver.

Ned had indeed been through a very similar devastation only the year before, when he'd caught his girlfriend, who went by her childhood nickname, Binky, in flagrante with a younger, more studly actor. Said stud was, according to Ned, one of those actors who at some point in every part they played took off their shirt to reveal their outstandingly buff chest. Fortysomething

Ned, though in great shape, could never compete with a twenty-five-year-old Obsession ad. Ned felt cut off at the knees or slightly higher. Sessions with a couples' therapist ensued; Binky's indiscretions with the Stud continued. Finally, Ned and Binky broke up. The story made its glum way back from L.A., where Ned and Binky had been holed up auditioning for second-rate television dramas, an unhappy object lesson about the perils of pilot season and youthful pects.

When I finally peeled myself off the floor and put away all the contents of the Balducci's basket, I decided I had to get out of my apartment to see the final dress rehearsal for the play Ned was directing. I felt very fragile and wispy as I trudged over in the freezing January air, as though the slightest gust could send me careening toward the Hudson River.

When I got to my seat at the back of the theater, I felt a tender squeeze on my right shoulder. It was Ned, his expression full of solicitude.

"Blue skies are coming. They're right around the corner."

"When?" I pleaded, seriously hoping Ned knew the exact timeline.

"Real soon," he assured me slowly, the way you do when you're talking to a child or a crazy person. "Six months? You'll see." He smiled warmly. "You'll be OK. More than OK—you'll be just *great*."

I wanted to believe him, needed to believe him, unmoored as I was, and I hung on to those words for weeks afterward. I found myself looking forward to his class again, and also to his daily morning call to see how I was doing. He invited me to lunch at Whole Wheat N' Wild Berries, a macrobiotic restaurant on Tenth Street, to try a seitan dish that was supposed to taste like boeuf bourguignon, then cajoled me into helping him pick paint for his apartment ("There are so many fucking whites!"). He brought a sage smudge stick over to my apartment and encouraged me to burn it and wave the smoke around my windows and doors ("It'll get rid of the bad vibes from being fucked over"). He even bought me a massage—my first—at a wondrous little place on Sixteenth Street called Carapan. A dark warren of groovy Santa Fe–ish rooms, redolent of cedar and sandalwood, tricked out with dream catchers and wind chimes, Carapan was noted for being "one of the only places to find quiet in the City." People spoke in whispers and padded around barefoot in fluffy robes while drinking hot apple cider; the only sound was Native American flute music that floated plaintively through hidden speakers. For ninety minutes, I lay inert on the table, sobbing, transported by the piped-in tom-toms.

"I used to cry all the time too," Ned confessed later, when I called to thank him. He sighed, then said absently, "Binky always loved that place . . ."

I was starting to grow really fond of Ned—how could I not? He was cool, smart, funny, generous, talented. We had a history. *A history.*

One night, I got a call from the stage manager of the new play in which Ned was starring.

"It's Ned's birthday. We're having a cake for him after the show, and I know he'd love to see you. Can you come by?"

*I know he'd love to see you.* Something about this was unnerving. Was it her tone? I kept replaying it in my mind, wondering. What was Ned telling her about me? Who *was* I to him? When I arrived backstage for the blowing out of the candles, the mostly female company and crew beamed at me beatifically.

"Ohhhhh! *Hiiiiiii!*"

"It's *very* nice to meet you!"

"Soooo *glad* you could make it! Let me get you a *chair*!"

"I *love* your coat!"

"Hey, you," Ned said, giving me a hug. His gaze was doe-eyed, his tone boyfriendy. "So glad to see you . . ."

Jesus Christ. When had we turned the corner? Only weeks before, I had been dumped by the guy I'd thought I was going to spend my life with. I had told Ned about my desolation, how hard it all was, and how I couldn't trust anyone again, so what was with the sudden pushiness? It seemed starkly different from the way he'd been behaving since my breakup. Or had I been so absorbed by my own anguish that I was only now noticing what he had been like all along? No, I decided. This was definitely different.

"Where are you?" Ned murmured, love light in his eyes. "You seem a million miles away."

"I . . . I, uh . . . you know, I'm just—"

"Tired?" Ned rubbed my shoulders sympathetically.

"Yeah, I'm really tired. I'm—I'm gonna go—OK?"

"Sure. Go get some sleep. We'll talk in the morning. Thanks for coming."

"Oh, yeah, sure," I said as I walked to the stage door, calling bye over my shoulder to the Cabal of Yentas Who Knew Everything.

"Bye!" they sang out affectionately. "See you *soon!*"

Walking home, I struggled to figure out how I felt. Was I even attracted to Ned? I was—kind of. He was one of those "real guys" who did "guy things" like carpentry and camping and shooting pistols, yet at the same time he had an equanimity about him, a watery, offbeat, artistic side. I liked this; it was a hot combo. I loved watching him onstage, too. He had this uncanny grace, the way he moved about the space, even when he was just demonstrating something in class. He was electrifying.

Also, there was the hippie thing; I'd always had a soft spot for hippies. All my babysitters in the seventies were hippies and I was obsessed with them. There was Julie, who wrote her class notes on her feet instead of using paper; Sherry, who told me she'd rather be dead than thirty; and Vicky, whose bitten-to-the-quick nails and schoolmarmish glasses belied the frenzied rendition of Joplin's "Piece of My Heart" she would perform on demand. On Saturday evenings, the moment my parents were out the door, I'd encourage whichever hippie babysitter was "on" that night to invite over her boyfriend—or "old man," as they always referred to them—so I could watch them make out. I'd sit beside them on the floor, *Mary Tyler Moore* or *The Bob Newhart Show* blaring in the background, while they lay barefoot on the couch, wrapped up in each other's hair, smoking joints. During commercials, I'd serve them Entenmann's Fudge Brownies and Cheez Doodles and Coke and tell them about my dreams.

Maybe it was the weed, but they always seemed so *interested*. They listened to me intently, as though I were some kind of prophet.

"Far out . . ." they'd repeat. These people were fantastic; they always made me feel like I was OK.

But . . . the Pass still made me uneasy. However absurd it may have felt at this point, I just couldn't ignore it. It was like an alarm buzzer or a yeast infection.

Ned called the next morning to make plans for dinner, since it was Monday, his day off from the play. This would be our first time having dinner; we had thus far seen each other exclusively during daylight. He suggested John's, an Italian restaurant in the East Village. His vibe on the phone was disquietingly datelike. Also, John's was well known as one of those Very Romantic Places—incredibly dark and lit only by what seemed like thousands of candles, erotically dripping white wax. It was adored for its cheap Chianti and fabulous spaghetti and meat-balls, both of which were hungrily sucked and slurped by hip-sters in a pre-sex haze.

I decided that this was an opportunity to set Ned straight about everything. I needed to tell him (a) that I was not in a place to jump into another "thing"; (b) that I was feeling pushed and that if there *was* the possibility of a "thing" with him, it would have to evolve organically, and my timeline and pace would have to be respected; and (c) after all these years, how I felt about the Pass.

"Gosh, you look great! What a delightful skirt!" Ned gushed as we got settled and started perusing the menu. "I've always said you look so pretty when you dress like a girl." As cool as Ned was, he also had an archaically corny side to him that gave off the whiff of a closet sexist. While he applauded the fact that I had "a mouth like a sailor" and was thoroughly impressed with the vigor with which I uttered the phrase "Fuck you," he couldn't contain his belief that, in the end, I should "act and dress like a girl." It pissed me off royally whenever he brought it up, but he was always careful to couch it as something I should experiment with "to get acting gigs."

Ned and I ordered spaghetti and meatballs, a mixed salad, and Chianti, and as we ate I felt him staring at me.

"Ned, listen, I'm—can I talk to you about a couple things?"

"Of course! Shoot."

"Well . . . it's just that I'm feeling . . . *pushed*. Like, I'm sort of getting the vibe that you might be wanting something . . . more. More than I can . . . commit to. And you know how fucked up I've been. I'm just—I'm not in a place—"

"Naw, naw . . ." Ned put down his Chianti and grabbed my hands and looked directly, intensely into my eyes. I could tell he was pretty stoned.

"We are totally *copacetic*, you and me." But he winced a bit, and that's when I saw it for the first time: the chink in Ned's armor. Beneath the smile, the mettle, the ballsy confidence, Ned seemed scared—but of what? He pressed on, cajoling me and convincing himself.

"We're pals, you and me—great pals!"

Taking a deep breath, I pressed on.

"Look, Ned. I wanna talk to you about something else, and it's pretty huge and weird and . . . it's hard. This is hard for me."

"I'm all ears."

I took another deep breath.

"Remember what happened that night seven years ago, after we had dinner together and we went back to your place to hang and sing some songs?"

"Uh . . . no," Ned smiled. "Should I?"

"We went back to your place. After the Westbank Cafe. We went back to your place, and we sat on the couch, and you started playing that tune by The Band . . ."

Ned looked at me blankly.

"Yeah?" He shrugged.

"So—none of this is ringing a bell?"

He shook his head.

"OK, well, did it ever occur to you *why* I stopped speaking to you for seven years?"

"You stopped speaking to me?" Ned looked perplexed. "I just thought we, you know, fell out of touch. I was with Binky and, you know . . ."

"Right. You were with Binky. You were also with Binky when you made a pass at me in your apartment seven years ago."

"What?"

"Binky was out of town," I continued. "You invited me over. We were on your couch. You were playing guitar and started singing that tune 'Take a load off Fannie'?"

"'The Weight'! Fuck! SUCH a GREAT tune!" Ned started singing, conducting with his fork. "'*And! (And!) (And!) You put the load right on ME-ee-ee!*'"

"Right. Anyway, we were on the couch, you sang a couple choruses, then stopped, turned to me, and said, 'Now I'm going to make a pass at you,' and stuffed your tongue in my mouth. Coming back to you now?"

Ned thought for a minute, spaced-out, glassy-eyed.

"You know, honestly, I don't remember. I remember that we kissed once and it was fucking great. But, you know me and the details." He laughed. "One of the drawbacks of pot, you know . . ."

"Well, let me refresh your memory. You made a pass at me. You made a pass at me, and afterward I pretty much fled. And, by the way, whenever I told the Jazz Musician about what happened between you and me, he always pointed out that after you shoved your tongue in my mouth, I did, in fact, continue making out with you, as opposed to, say, biting it off or pushing you away or kneeing you in the nuts, so it's not like I don't recognize that I was *there* and culpable—sort of—since I *did* keep kissing you back for whatever it was, five minutes? But the point is that I was confused. I was young. You were my teacher and my friend, and I really looked up to you. You'd just directed me in that awesome play, which got me all kinds of attention, so, I dunno, maybe a part of me was intrigued. But a bigger part of me was freaked out, especially when you maneuvered us over to your brass bed under the dimmed track lights, where slung over the bedpost was Binky's white silk negligee. And I asked; 'What about Binky?' And you said, 'She's in Philadelphia.'

Huh? *What did that even mean*? That once she was across state lines, all bets were off?"

"I don't know . . . I don't remember," Ned sighed. "But I think we had a different *arrangement* back then."

"Really? 'Cause I seriously doubt that Binky would have been psyched to see what was going down—"

"I don't know about 'psyched,' but she'd be maybe—"

"Pissed. Pissed is how she would have been, Ned. Let's face it. And then I was, you know, all discombobulated, and you started telling me how you had always been attracted to me—"

"Well, that's true."

"And I felt all fucked up 'cause I thought you actually thought I was *talented* and thought I was a *good actor*—"

"So? I *did* think that—"

"But really, in the end, all you wanted to do was fuck me—"

"Hey! Now that's not fair. Wanting to fuck you doesn't preclude my admiring your talent, you know. I think you're damn good, your *winsomeness* notwithstanding."

"OK, but it made me feel terrible. And dirty and wrong. Especially when you told me you wanted to have a thing with me *while* you were still with Binky! Like a Mormon!"

"What can I say—I dug you both."

"What in the fuck would make you think I'd be willing to go halvsies? That any chick would? Anyway, we made out a little more. You took my shirt off and then your own and flung back the covers. Which is when I saw—on the perfectly crisp, five-hundred-count, Egyptian-blah-blah, white cotton sheets—a teeny, tiny speck of blood. Binky's blood. On the sheets, staring right up at me."

"I definitely don't remember this part . . ."

"And you go, 'Oh, shit, Binky musta had her period or something. I'll just get a new sheet,' and I go—and I know it's all very soap opera–y, but I was twenty—I go, 'You can't just throw Binky into the hamper, Ned. Binky is *here*.' Then I got up, put my shirt on, and asked for cab money, and you said, 'You're really gonna split, huh?' And I said, 'Yeah, I really am. I don't wanna be just another bloodstain on your sheets.' Which really is a pretty good exit line for a kid. And then I left, and we didn't speak again till I signed up for your class a few months ago."

"Wow. I'm just . . . floored."

"I know it all seems really melodramatic in retrospect, but Ned, you know, I was very, very fucked up about that."

"I hear ya . . ."

"And I have to be honest with you about this, about how I felt about what went down between us. If we're gonna be 'pals.' It's not easy to even talk about it, and I've spent years feeling awful because you meant a lot to me, you know? I was incredibly disillusioned and, quite frankly, I also felt really ashamed."

Ned sat motionless, looking supremely chastened.

We sat there for a few minutes, staring at each other. I was exhausted from the confession yet felt enormous relief at having unburdened myself to him.

"I am just . . . ugh . . . what can I say? I am so, so SORRY. I mean—UGH!" Ned, full of remorse, rocked back and forth in his chair and kept thrusting his head into his hands on the table.

"I'm desperate here," he blurted, dolefully.

"Well, look, don't be desperate. This is good. We needed to clear the air."

"What can I do?"

"What do you mean?"

"I am so—SO SORRY!" He took my hands. "Do you even REALIZE how SORRY I am? How can I make it up to you? How?"

"Look, I don't—"

"I just hate that something like this has been hanging over our heads. We're such *great pals*, you and me. We have SO MUCH in common, you know? We—our *souls*—are connected in a really, REALLY cool way. Past-life shit, possibly. Who knows? And I'd hate to think that I'd somehow, inadvertently fucked up our swell friendship!"

One of the candles on our table burned out, and Ned quickly relit it with his Bic. Once we were again sufficiently illuminated, Ned offered to take me up to his cabin in Maine. We would leave, he suggested, that Sunday, the day after his show closed, for a week as a sort of peace offering, a kind of burying-the-hatchet-type oblation, meant to wash away the old and inaugurate our newfound adult camaraderie.

"Ned," I said, "you know how much you mean to me, how much I appreciate everything you've done for me and how great you've been, how great you *are*. It's just, I can't be in a 'thing,' and I can't feel like that's what you're angling for. What I really want—what I really need—is a friend. It's amazingly generous of you to offer, but . . . I think it would be weird at this point. I totally appreciate—"

"I know, I know, I know," he soothed. "But—can I just say something here? This would be a trip as *pals*. Nothing more. No pressure, no weirdness. I want to do this, just so I can give this to you. It's that *simple*. Totally on the level, totally *copacetic*. Just to make up for . . . for the thing that happened. So that it doesn't fuck us up with hard feelings and stuff. So we can move on. Really."

Ned put his hand over his heart and two fingers in the air. "Scout's honor."

His smile was unfeigned, and the candlelight deepened the crow's-feet around his eyes, making him seem strangely vulner-

able. I pictured him as he must have been twenty-five years before: long blond hair, open, boyish. Still stoned, but less fried;
wicked yet unsullied by the bitterness that would later engulf
him when disillusionment set in. Watching his buddies get ahead
of him, his marriages crumble, the world become more uptight
instead of less. I felt incredibly sad, not just for Ned, but for me,
too. Tears came to my eyes.

"Whatsa matter, Nance?" Ned said genuinely concerned.
"You know, I'm being sincere, right? I would never just use
'Scout's honor' in vain—you know that, right?"

"I do know that, Ned." I felt such affection for him right
then and such hope that perhaps now our relationship could
enter a new phase, one of true friendship. It all made me feel so
hopeful at a time when cynicism had overtaken me. "We will be
friends for a long time," I thought.

"You're sure? I just don't want to have it be weird. And, like,
confusing, you know . . . *at night*."

"Totally sure!" Ned said.

"I mean, no hanky-panky."

"Hey, you be Hanky and I'll be Panky! Wait! No, I'll be
Hanky and you . . ." He smiled. "Kidding. Look: you'll have
your own room, and I won't lay a hand on you. What d'ya say?
Deal?"

I had misgivings, but getting out of the city did sound good.
It was March, the most depressing and gray part of the winter.
Going north to Maine, with its fresh air and slower pace, did
have its allure. Why not? I had been clear with Ned; we were
"copacetic."

"Can we watch the Oscars? They're on Sunday night, and I
wanna see if Marisa Tomei wins."

"You betcha!"

"Deal," I said. "Thank you so much!"

I don't know why, exactly, I felt the need to stipulate Marisa Tomei as part of the agreement. I didn't even *know* Marisa Tomei, though she floated in some of the same downtown theater crowds as both Ned and I. Occasionally, I'd see her at a party or at a mutual friend's late-night gig, always laughing, looking beautiful across the room. While I did want to watch the Oscars, my insistence had more to do with the desire for a linchpin. It was something to hang on to.

When I climbed into Ned's gleaming pickup truck early that Sunday morning for our six-hour journey, he was seated behind the wheel in his Maine Getup: a chamois shirt, a lumberjack jacket, and rubber all-weather boots. His hair was gelled, and he held a bouquet of yellow tulips.

"Yellow means 'friendship,' " he smiled sheepishly, turning up the radio. "Well, off like a prom dress!"

The highlight of our road trip was singing along with Ned's sixties mix tape. The greatest hits of Crosby, Stills, Nash and Young; Peter, Paul and Mary; Buffalo Springfield; the Doobie Brothers—Ned singing lead and me taking the harmony parts. Busting out on all these tunes, we couldn't help occasionally laughing at their mannered histrionics and all the overwrought beseeching.

> *There's somethin' happenin' here*
> *What it is ain't exactly clear*

We cruised up the highway, levitating in some musically induced reverie that delivered us from bleakness. After six hours, I was feeling infinitely better and immensely grateful to Ned for the time we had shared. He was right: this was exactly what I needed, we were great pals, and I was lucky to have him in my life. Once we were within a few miles of Ned's place, we stopped for provisions at a little market, cracking up as we gamely selected a variety of pesticide-free veggies, additive-free grains, and biodegradable products.

"Hey, look!" I said, pointing to a small hemp sack while we waited in line to pay for our things. "It's couscous. Did I tell you? It's my new favorite thing!"

"Wanna get some?" Ned asked. Damn! This was *fun*. And easy. Easy-peasy. Blue skies. What the hell had I been so worried about?

"Here we are!"

Ned grinned, flinging open the door to his cabin and steering me over the threshold. I looked around. The cabin, which is perhaps too generous a term—let's call it a shanty—was one long room. There was a kitchen on the right side, and on the left was a full-size bed with a fluffy white down comforter adorned with a richly hued handwoven Native American blanket. Completing the mise-en-scène was a black potbellied stove, which stood majestically in the middle of the space. The air was thick with cedar.

"This is great, Ned. It's really beautiful."

"Thanks," he said, pulling me to him. "I was hoping you'd dig it." He gave me a light peck on the lips and brushed the hair out of my face. "You sure are *fetching*. Mint tea?"

Uh-oh. Scanning the room, trying not to panic, I saw a door on the left side, adjacent to the bed. Was that the other room? Where else would it be?

"I just—maybe I'll just throw my stuff—"

"Just throw it on the bed," Ned said, filling the kettle. "You don't have to unpack this minute."

I knew before I knew, and yet still, I had to ask.

"So. Where's . . . ?"

He looked at me, a total blank.

"Where's . . . what?"

"The other . . . ?"

Still blank.

"The other what?"

Oh. My. Fucking. God.

"The other room." And then, very quietly, very small, like Cindy Lou Who in *The Grinch*, "My room."

Ned eyed me quizzically. "I'm not sure what you mean. Here"—he handed me my tea—"you should let it steep a bit." He smiled warmly. "So. What d'ya say I start a nice big fire and you start rustling us up some grub?"

"You gotta be kidding. WHERE THE FUCK IS MY BED?" I demanded. "You SAID there was another bed—WHERE IS IT?"

Ned did a double take, flabbergasted.

"Now hold on there," His benevolent aura evaporated. "I don't appreciate your tone."

"Yeah? Well, I don't appreciate being LIED to."

" 'Lied to'? You're calling me a *liar*?"

He put his tea down and turned to face me, blood boiling. "You need to calm down and get ahold of yourself."

"Ned, you said there would be another bed—WAIT! NO! You said there'd be another whole room! For me! To stay in so it wouldn't be weird! But guess what? It's pretty fucking weird! Weirder than I could have even imagined!"

"Now listen to me: I never, ever said there was another bed. I never said there was another room. You know why I never said those things? 'CAUSE I DON'T HAVE THOSE THINGS."

"This is totally fucked up . . ."

"You want to know what's really fucked up? YOU. And all

those women like you. *Mind games.* Playing major *mind games.*
You came up here—*willingly*—you came here to be with me. You
knew what this was, and you made a decision, on your own.
You are a grown woman, and you said, '*I'm gonna go up to
Ned's cabin for a week, with Ned.*' Now, who's fucking with
whose head?"

I was so astonished that I could only stand there mutely,
blinking at him in dazed bewilderment.

"HOW DARE YOU?" he continued, ranting, now swollen
with indignation and pomposity. "How dare you turn this into
a scenario in which YOU have been bamboozled when, in fact,
it is ME who has been taken advantage of? I feel amorous toward you. This was to be romantic, and you have led me on."

"Ned. I told you, I said it clearly, and you said you understood. I am NOT ready for something to be a thing and—"

"Then you shouldn't have come here! You shouldn't have accepted the invitation of a man who you know has feelings for
you. It is *wrong*, and it is *manipulative*."

"How is it manipulative when you agreed that we could
come as friends?"

"You *really* are a woman, aren't you? This is what women do
all the time."

"Do what? What do 'women do'?"

"Change their minds. They change their minds. They have all
that *power*. They know if a guy likes them, has feelings for them,
buys them dinner, flowers, massages . . . Does that translate into
maybe wanting a little pussy? YES, AND SO WHAT? This is a
genuine *courting* going on. No one in their right mind would
have ever construed this as anything but. I WAS COURTING
YOU, Ma'am! To accept those things, knowing I was fucking
*courting you*, well, that is just awful."

"Seriously, Ned, what fucking century are we in? You were

'COURTING ME'? What is this—*Gone with the Wind*? You may have felt you were 'COURTING ME' and that you had the right to do so without asking me if that was OK with me—"

"See? This is how all those terrible women get away with their sexual harassment nonsense!"

"OK. I am not about to discuss the politics of gender mores with you, Ned. The point is this was to be a trip *as friends*. You knew I was a mess. You knew I was heartbroken, and I told you, really clearly: I am not in any kind of shape to entertain a new relationship—"

"THEN WHY THE FUCK ARE YOU HERE?"

"Let. Me. FINISH!" I screamed back. "I told you where I was at, and you said—YOU. SAID. 'That's fine.' 'We are pals.' 'No pressure, no weirdness.' This is what you said. I expressed concern about coming to Maine maybe being a mixed message, and you go, 'Naw! We are *copacetic*.' Now, I don't even really know what the fuck that means, 'copacetic,' but I inferred by your usage that it meant we—you—were cool with being 'pals' and nothing more. Or is 'copacetic' another word for 'It's time for you to suck my dick'?"

Ned shook his head despondently, victimized.

"I think you coming here," he said, "knowing how attracted I am to you, how I have always had a crush on you . . . well, to shine me on like that . . ."

I sat down at the table next to the kitchen and examined the grooves in the planks.

"I just feel so taken advantage of. I really thought you were being my friend. Just like I thought you were being my friend when I was hanging out in your apartment and you made a pass at me—"

"So this is what it is," Ned looked like Jack Lord, unearthing the big crime plot point on *Hawaii Five-O*. "You're getting me back. Now that I'm in a vulnerable spot, having been *cuckolded* by Binky, you're getting me back—"

"Jesus Christ, Ned, you are infuriating! How can you so deftly turn this around and make me the villain? It's all about you and how you've been fucked over."

I got up, grabbed my cigarettes, and stepped onto the porch to fire one up. Ned followed. He wasn't done.

"I just think it's really *disingenuous* of you to come up to a man's place when you know he likes you. You should have known that back then, too, incidentally. But look, I don't want to fight anymore. I'm exhausted from the long drive, I'm hungry, and I'm sad. Terribly sad."

I stared off the porch, zoning out, in the direction of Ned's truck. It was parked in the mud. The right front tire seemed to be sinking.

"I'm sorry you're sad, Ned. I don't know what to say at this point." I finished my cig and butted it out.

"Here," Ned held open the palm of his hand. "I'll take it." He stared at the cigarette butt for a few seconds, rolling it around in his fingers before letting out an audible, exasperated sigh. "I guess it's just a big misunderstanding. Should we make something to eat? I'm starved and spent."

"Sure. Sure. Why don't I make us some veggie couscous, you make a fire, and we can eat dinner and watch the Oscars—how does that sound?"

"Sounds great, 'cept for one minor detail."

"What's that?"

"I don't have a TV."

So. Ned didn't have a TV. No guest bed, no TV, and another thing Ned didn't have, which he'd also failed to mention: a bathroom. Actually, he *had* a bathroom. It's just that it was *outside*. Ned's bathroom was an outhouse.

I always hated *Little House on the Prairie*. Hated the show, hated the books. Hated "Half Pint" and all those boring "lessons" elucidated by Michael Landon about long winters and bad crops and what happens to people who have hate in their hearts. But what really seemed like the most disgusting thing ever about *Little House on the Prairie* was the fact that they had to go to the bathroom in an outhouse. I just couldn't fathom it. Even *The Waltons* had plumbing.

To find myself in the revolting predicament of having to shit in a hole was almost, given what else had transpired, too much to bear. Maybe it's just me, but it seemed amazing that Ned thought that taking a chick for a woo-pitching wingding up to a shack with an *outhouse* for a bathroom was a no-brainer in terms of romance. In addition, I don't even remotely have an air about me that might suggest I'm the type who enjoys "roughing it." You could hardly persuade me to have a picnic in Central Park; I don't camp or have a mess kit. I get grossed out at almost every public restroom and even at the homes of some of my friends—so why, *why*, was there no mention of the outhouse? I decided, rather impractically, that I wouldn't pee or shit until I spotted, on the horizon, the Fifty-ninth Street Bridge. But with all the roughage we were consuming, that plan lasted about forty-five minutes.

The outhouse was straightforward enough: a wooden half shed, with a swinging latch door and a hole in the ground. I don't remember if there was something you actually put your ass on; there must have been, but all I remember is the hole. I remember that it was March, it was freezing, and there was a hole. That night, I lay awake in bed, plagued by the lacerating voice of my old roommate, Therese, who had correctly predicted the catastrophic heartbreak I would suffer at the calloused hands of the Jazz Musician, and who had also so pithily described her views on my flaws of character and wanton shamelessness.

"COCK-TEASE!" she'd squawked. "TWAT-TEASE!"

In the quiet of the frigid, moonless night, as I lay motionless, fully clothed under the covers, I heard Therese and her vituperations.

"BITCH!"

"WHORE!"

"YOUR FAULT YOUR FAULT, YOUR FAULT, YOUR FAULT!"

At some point, I drifted off. When I woke in the morning, Ned was up, sitting in his flannel robe, drinking tea in front of the stove, listening to Garrison Keillor.

"She won," he said absently.

"What?"

"Marisa. She won."

"Wow—really?" I clapped my hands together; I was elated. I tried to picture her: her expression when they announced her name, her dress, her hair, what she ate afterward, what she was doing right now, at that moment. "Oh my god. She did it!"

"Yup," Ned replied, glumly. I wished so bad that I could have seen it, and though I knew someone must have taped it, I also knew I'd never actually sit down to watch it. The moment, for whatever reason, had passed. Watching it after the fact would only highlight what I had missed.

"There's hot water in the kettle," Ned said. "Want some tea?"

"I would, thanks."

Ned puttered over to the stove while I sat down at the table. He handed me my tea, then rolled a joint, got stoned, and went out for a two-mile run. When he came back, he was in better spirits and scarfed down two heaping bowls of Grape-Nuts cereal. I sat across from him while he ate.

"Ned," I said finally, "I am really sorry if you felt led on. Really, really sorry. I tried to be clear as best I could."

"OK," he said, pouting.

"I'm also upset, though, 'cause I feel like you don't care about my feelings. You're on your own timeline, and whether I'm ready or not to date seems to be of no concern to you."

"Look, I told you: you have disappointed me with your *capriciousness*. You knew how I felt, and that's all I have to say."

"Is there any way we can shelve this for right now? Can we just agree to disagree? I mean—I thought we were friends. At the very least, aren't we friends?" I started to cry. Ned got up and handed me a dish towel.

"Come on, don't cry. Yes, we can be friends."

We decided to take a drive into town. It was a beautiful day, and a good deal warmer than the previous day. We walked around the main street for a bit and went to a little sandwich shop for lunch. At the register, they were selling *The Moosewood Cookbook*, and thumbing through it, I decided I wanted to get it.

"Let me get that for you," Ned offered, taking the book from me and pulling out his wallet.

"No, come on, I don't want you to do that, Ned," I protested.

"I want to," he insisted. "To make up for . . ." He sighed. "All of it. Just—this is on me."

"That's very sweet, thank you. Thank you very much."

When we got back to Ned's place that afternoon, the mud situation seemed to have worsened.

"Yup," Ned concurred when I mentioned it. "That's the thing about mud season: you can pull out of your driveway in the morning, and there's just a teensy bit of mud; you get home just a few hours later, and it's a quagmire."

The reason for this, Ned explained, was that as the winter faded into spring and the snow on the ground melted, the layers of ground lying deep below were still frozen, unable to absorb the water. The result was a slushy, muddy mess that engulfed the area's small trails and old dirt roads almost until summer. People were constantly getting trapped in their homes, too afraid to brave the mud, sometimes for weeks at a time. Or worse, they would get trapped in the ruts created by tires whose wheels had been spun during desperate attempts to escape.

"So, is that where the expression 'stuck in a rut' comes from?" I asked Ned as we maneuvered our way into his driveway.

"Probably," he smiled. As I then pondered that old saw "spinning your wheels," Ned grabbed my hand and looked meaningfully into my eyes. "What d'ya say I teach you how to shoot a pistol?"

The afternoon sun was bright, the sky a glorious azure, and as we listened to the Velvet Underground on a boom box, Ned taped several quarters to a wooden board and loaded a .357 Magnum. At Singing Oaks Day Camp, when I was eleven, I had taken riflery and been OK—nothing special. So I was pretty amazed to find out that I demonstrated a savantlike aptitude with a firearm. I was a great shot.

"Woo-hoo!" Ned hollered, running over to examine my handiwork. "Jesus Christmas, you nailed the fucker!"

Retrieving it from the board, he wiped it off on his jeans before handing it to me for inspection. George Washington's face was grossly disfigured, the bullet's force having smooshed and splattered it. The quarter was concave, as though it were about to fold in half.

"You should keep that thing with you for luck," Ned commented wryly.

We continued to blast coins to a fare-thee-well until almost sundown.

"That was fucking great. I can't believe how fun that was," I told him as we put away the ammo and locked up the guns in his shed.

"You're a natural," he said, grinning.

"Well, you explained it really well and made it easy. You're a great teacher!"

"Aw, shucks," he said, laughing, pretending to be bashful. "But seriously, you are pretty goddamn good with a gun. Thing is, most girls are usually better shots than guys, but you are pretty amazing even still."

"Why is that—that girls are better?"

" 'Cause they're calmer. When they know they have the shot lined up and they're ready to pull the trigger, they just know how to breathe into it, staying steady. It's innate. Guys get too pumped; they got too much adrenaline or testosterone or something. Fucks 'em up every time . . ."

We went back to the cabin, and I lay on the bed to read a bit before we figured dinner out. Ned put some wood on the fire and, after a minute or two, joined me on the bed with a book of his own. Then he made another pass at me. I was now officially in some sort of existential hell, experiencing an endless loop of the same scene.

"Ned. No."

He threw his book across the room.

"NO AGAIN, HUH? NO AGAIN?" He was in a full-blown rage. "How long is this going to last? How long are you going to put me through this?"

"Put you through what?"

"I just don't get you. You really are something. WHY DID YOU COME HERE?"

"Ned—please. Calm down!"

"GODDAMN YOU! YOU KNEW WHAT THIS WAS! YOU KNEW THAT I WAS SHOPPING!"

"*Shopping?*"

"THAT'S RIGHT! SHOPPING," he screamed. "SHOPPING FOR A WOMAN! YOU KNEW THAT AND YOU HAVE WASTED MY FUCKING TIME!"

I sat on the edge of the bed, stunned, and wished to god I was still packing a loaded gun.

"Um . . . ? I hate to tell you this, but one doesn't SHOP FOR A WOMAN. This isn't a fucking Moroccan bazaar, Ned."

"You know what I mean!" he shouted.

"Actually I don't. And you know what else? I don't care. You haven't been listening. You haven't listened to one word."

Ned walked away, livid, and started rolling a joint, which he smoked as he put on his sneakers. When he was done, he went out for yet another stoned run. I was so mad that I was shaking. Standing on his porch, chain-smoking, I decided that I hated him. I grabbed the portable phone—the one piece of modern technology Ned's cave came equipped with—and called my best friend, Bridget, back in New York and told her the whole thing.

"He took me here under totally false pretenses!" I stormed. "I mean, I was completely duped into coming."

"I know, Nance, I know. Just take some deep breaths."

Almost a decade older than me, Bridget usually assumed the role of patient big sister or "mom we'd most like to have." Nothing much fazed her—especially when it came to complaints about men or families.

"I think," she continued gently, "you need to ask yourself why you're there."

"You mean—you think he's right? I shouldn't have come up here unless I was prepared to put out?"

Therese's voice popped back into my head: "*Yes, cunt! He's right! And you are a total whore! Your fault! Your fault! Your fault! Hahahahahaaaa!*"

"No, I mean in a more cosmic sense. I think we get ourselves into things all on our own. Yeah, he's a scumbag, or he's fucked up or, you know . . . has weird, archaic views of women. That's him; that's who he is. Most likely he won't change; it'd be like rerouting a river. Whatever. Forget about him for a sec. You are *there*. And you need to ask yourself why."

I started to cry.

"So, it *is* my fault. I fucked it all up. Again . . ."

"Now come on, that's just silly. There are no fuckups, Nance. Be better to yourself than that. All I'm sayin' is you can use this as an opportunity, a gift. You know? On a certain level, you knew what this was and what would happen. Yeah, you made a deal with him, some kind of 'contract' or some kind of 'out' clause about what this week would be, but in the end, *you went up there*. You made that decision. For yourself."

"But why?" I wailed, wishing I could Jeannie-blink myself into Bridget's lap. "What's the reason?"

Bridget sighed. I heard her lighting a cigarette.

"I think it's 'cause you don't want to be alone. None of us do. And I think you need to be a bit more unapologetic about your needs. I feel like your remorse over this is out of whack; you didn't wanna fuck him. Even if you did and you changed your mind—mid-fuck even—that would be your prerogative."

"I told him, though, Bridgie. I did. It was a big thing, too: to say my feelings and be honest and tell him what I needed and then—"

"Again, forget about him and what he did. Doesn't matter. You beat yourself up for just expressing yourself. You're so willing to accept the crumbs, and then you berate yourself with 'Oh! Maybe I took too much!' Know what I mean?"

She was right. I sat there crying, listening to her smoke on the other end, Buddy Holly warbling in the background. A few feet away from me, Ned's truck seemed to have sunk even further into the mud. It was lopsided now, the front dipping lower than the back.

"Nance?"

"Yeah. I'm just thinking."

" 'Bout what?"

"I was just remembering this time I went with my dad and brother and sister to visit my grandmother on Long Island."

"Uh-huh."

"It was a long trip—two hours or something—and on the way back, I had to pee, so I told my dad, 'I think I need to pee,' and he goes, 'Can you hold it?' and I go, 'Yeah.' "

"Mmmm-hmmm."

"I really needed to pee, Bridgie. Bad. But I knew, I just knew the right answer. The answer he wanted was 'Yeah, I can hold it.' But I couldn't hold it. I ended up peeing all over myself, and all I could think was god I hope I didn't get it on my father's car."

Bridget sighed.

"I'm so sorry, Nance."

"I must have been ten years old. Old enough not to be having accidents and peeing on myself."

"But this wasn't an accident. You knew what you needed, and you ignored it. And you know what, Nance?"

"What?"

"I think you might have a little pee on yourself right now, too."

"I know. You are so right. So, now what do I do?"

"Go change."

When Ned got back from his run, I told him I couldn't stay and had called and made a plane reservation to fly home that night. Ned agreed to drive me to the airport. But there were forces conspiring against me by now: the mud had reached biblical proportions. We spent an hour in Ned's driveway trying to steer the truck out of the mud, but it was hopeless; I was stuck. We called the local mud puller-outers, but they refused to come, saying that the mud was too severe and that they wouldn't be able to get to Ned's until the morning. The next morning, as we waited for them to come pull us out, I became frantic.

"Ned, I've got to get outta here. Please, I'm begging you. I've got to go!"

Ned got out of the truck and circled to the back, and I got behind the wheel, and somehow, after forty-five minutes, we were out of Ned's driveway and on our way to the airport. We drove in silence. After a while, Ned turned on the radio. The station started playing "The Weight."

> *I pulled into Nazareth, was feelin' about half past dead;*
> *I just need some place where I can lay my head.*

"I've always loved this tune," Ned said. He sang along softly, and I looked out the window at all the barren trees.

> *"Hey, mister, can you tell me where a man might find a bed?"*
> *He just grinned and shook my hand, and "No!" was all he said.*

On the chorus, Ned turned to me.

"Do you know what this song is about?" he asked.

"Um . . . yeah. It's about doing a favor for a friend. And

about, you know, sharing the burden or 'weight' of responsibility. Something like that."

Ned nodded, then furrowed his brow, reflecting.

"Actually, it's about a chick who gave a guy the clap."

"What?"

"Supposedly," he continued. "That was the rumor, anyway. That's what 'taking the load off Fannie' means."

I looked at him.

"Some chick gave some poor slob the clap," he sighed mournfully, shaking his head. "Oh, well. It's still a great song, huh?"

Well. It was quite an interpretation. That he *still* didn't remember singing "The Weight" to me in his apartment all those years before blew my mind, but I just had to laugh. Was it the pot that made him so hazy about the details of the past? Was it that, like a lot of people's, his memory was selective? Was it that he just didn't give a shit? Was "The Weight" really about the clap? Did it matter? I decided, in that moment, that no, it did not. What mattered was that I had learned to shoot a bullet through a quarter and I had made it out of the mud.

## 4. The Debra Winger Thing

**I used to** do a pretty impressive impersonation of Debra Winger.

During my NYU years, my friends and I used to hang out after rehearsals at this dive bar called Phebe's on Fourth Street, drinking warm beer and trying to outperform one another until dawn.

"Hey, Nance," someone would snicker. "Do the Debra Winger Thing!"

Rising from the lopsided table with a flourish, I'd begin.

"Remember the scene in *An Officer and a Gentleman* when Richard Gere is being an asshole after he gets into a fight with those townies at the bar, and then he and Winger are back at their motel room, and she's trying to get him to 'open up to her,' and he gets all pissed and goes,

'OK, what do you want? You wanna fuck? You wanna fuck? OK, take your clothes off, get on the bed, and I'll give you a good fuck.'

'Where's that comin' from? You know somethin', Zack? You ain't nothin' special. You treat women like whores, and if you ask me, you ain't got no chance bein' no officer!'"

Then I'd act like I was Winger, all fucked up and upset, running out of the motel room. My friends thought it was a scream; it always made them hysterical, no matter how many times they'd seen it, despite the fact that I always did it the exact same way. As much as I enjoyed making them laugh, I never thought about it that much. To me, it was just a dopey little gag I would do when people were drunk or stoned, occasionally trotting it out for an audition, like I had for *Remote Control*. But time moved on, and as my school days faded into the distance, so, too, did the Debra Winger Thing, becoming one of those fun things I used to do—like tap dancing—that I no longer did, simply because no one ever asked.

Shortly after I turned twenty-eight, I was cast in an off-Broadway production of the Molière play *The Ridiculous Précieuses*, at the Kaufman Theatre. The production was bankrolled by our leading lady, who happened to be an heiress of one of our country's great, philanthropic, robber baron families. She had Philip Morris as a backer, so in addition to our Equity minimum salaries, the cast were offered as many packs of cigarettes as we could smoke a day. Undeterred by the homicidal innuendo, we all graciously accepted the producers' largesse.

I was thrilled to land this job, but the production was a mess. The Leading Lady, who had precious little acting experience, could say her lines and walk across the stage, but never at the same time. The director was a willowy blond from L.A. with fabulous clothes and scant directing credits. The Leading Lady and the director were best friends from college and loved each other "like sisters." Frequently, rehearsals were interrupted for various conflicts and tantrums, and the phrase "Fuck off, bitch" was bandied about with far more conviction than any of Molière's hilarious dialogue.

On one of these impromptu rehearsal breaks, I got to know Billy, who was to become one of my best friends. A squabble had erupted over the pronunciation of the word "inexorable."

"It's 'in-EX-orable!' " the director admonished.

"No, it's 'in-ex-OR-able!' " the Leading Lady insisted.

"Fuck off, bitch!"

"No, *you* fuck off, bitch!"

And the cast was dismissed for the better part of four hours.

Billy was a well-trained thespian from Texas who was living with Bobby Lewis, the theater legend who had been part of the original Group Theatre and cofounded the Actors Studio. Billy had turned a two-week internship with Bobby into a full-time domestic arrangement, wherein Billy saw to the substantial and constant needs of a cantankerous, partially deaf, eighty-year-old theater director and gained entrée into the rapidly disappearing world of the New York stage in its heyday.

Billy introduced me to Robin, an agent at a big Hollywood firm, who would later coax me out to Los Angeles to meet casting directors and audition for sitcoms. In nostalgic moments, Billy and I now refer to *The Ridiculous Précieuses* as the beginning of "our Lunt-Fontanne years."

One night, my parents drove in from Connecticut to see the play. I met them afterward at Chez Josephine, a restaurant I adored for its dramatic crystal chandeliers and crimson walls festooned with nude pictures of Josephine Baker. The proprietor was one of Baker's adopted sons, Jean-Claude, who had a penchant for the color red that extended even to his toenail polish. Billy and I frequently went to Chez Josephine for postshow drinks, so Jean-Claude made a big deal when he saw me, sweetly seating us under one of my favorite topless pictures of his mom.

"Well, that was just *brutal*," my father said after our entrées had arrived and the piano player had begun a Kander and Ebb medley.

"Aren't you ashamed to be in this piece of shit? Aren't you

just *humiliated*? These people are so *god-awe-ful*, and as usual, I didn't *undah-stand* what anyone was sayin'. What can come of this? I mean, really—what? You seem like a *lose-ah* working with such people. Seriously."

My mother sat mutely sipping her Scotch sour on the rocks, turned toward the window looking onto Forty-second Street, as if she'd forgotten something a long time ago.

I stared into my plate of Spaghetti Josephine, searching for meaning in the swirls of orange-mottled angel hair and flecks of Bolognese, but found only a face that looked a lot like an Edvard Munch painting.

I tried to explain that a life in the theater was a process; it was hard work, and really, I didn't think it was my place to judge this production—or any of the cast and crew—since I was trying to accumulate credits and gain experience. I told him that "work begets work," and that invariably I would get parts because someone saw me in something, and even if it was something bad, it would lead to me getting hired for another something. I told him that I felt lucky that they'd hired me.

Admittedly, the play was a colossal disaster, and everyone knew it. In an effort to micromanage the response of people who'd sat through ninety minutes of abuse, the director and the Leading Lady made the ushers hand out roses for the audience to toss out toward the cast during our curtain call. And yet, I loved it. I knew it sucked royally, but I loved it all the same. How could I not? I was *in New York. Acting onstage. With Billy.*

"And anyway," I told my father, with as much sangfroid as possible, "I met an agent from doing this crappy thing, and she wants me to come out to L.A. for a week. So, see? You just never know. Just like Mamet said, it's the old poker adage 'You can't win if you don't play.' "

"Ugh, Mamet," my father waved me off and signaled for the check. "Christ, this Mamet's a real *beaut*, lemme tell ya. If he's so great, how come he doesn't give you a goddamn job? Poker, he's teaching her. Maybe he'd like to pay y'rent?"

I got home that night and sat on the floor in my underwear, staring at myself in front of the full-length mirror attached to my bedroom closet door, crying and smoking my free cigarettes.

At three A.M., as I was dozing off, the phone rang. It was my old friend Sam, now a cast member on *Saturday Night Live.*

"Hey, Goofy, you still doin' the Debra Winger Thing? I want you to do it right now, over the phone for Phil Hartman. NBC's giving him a deal to do his own show, and I told him you should be the chick. 'Kay, ready?"

"Uh . . . yeah, I'm . . . yeah."

"Phil, pick up."

So, I did it over the phone for Phil Hartman.

"Nancy, what would you say if I told you I might have a job that will change your life?"

"I'd say, 'Oh my god, I've been waiting my whole life for someone to say that to me.' "

"Can you meet me here on Saturday at two?"

I arrived at the appointed time and was whisked via elevator to Studio 8-H. The place looked like it hadn't been refurbished since the seventies, when the original Not Ready for Prime Time Players first stumbled in. It was actually my third time at the fabled studio. The first was six years before with my friend Jane, rehearsing bit parts that would never make it to air; a couple years later, I was there with the Jazz Musician, when the band he was in was the musical guest. Both times I felt merely peripheral, incidental—would this time be the charm?

Phil met me and took me to his dressing room. I did the Debra

Winger Thing for him in person, and over the next hour he had me improvise some others.

"You're a voice actor, like me! This is great!"

He explained that the network had given him a development deal and that he'd originally wanted Jan Hooks to do the show with him, but she didn't want to leave New York, and the show was to shoot in Los Angeles.

"Sam suggested you, and for Sam to suggest any girl for *any-thing* . . ." Phil laughed. "Well, I suppose we all know what a big deal that is, right?"

It was true: Sam, like most of the male comics I knew, hated "comedy chicks." Whenever I made him laugh, he'd look at me with amazement and say, "Holy shit! You're *funny*! And chicks are just not funny, *ever* . . ."

At the end of my meeting with Phil, he walked me over to Sam's dressing room.

"I'm going to need you to meet some people. How can I get ahold of you? Your agent?"

For the first time that day I felt nervous. How could I tell Phil, who was in a froth over how "terrific" I was, about my pathetic representation situation? While technically I *did* have an agent, she was a malevolent troll named Sandy, who worked out of her mother's apartment on the Upper West Side and who, after sign-ing me when I'd gotten out of school, had never spoken to me again, except to inform me one afternoon that the casting direc-tor of *One Life to Live* had said I wasn't pretty enough to be "soapy."

In a burst of moxie, I told Phil I was actually trying to get out of my contract with my agent because I couldn't trust her.

"I just . . . see, the thing is . . . I don't want you to call me there, 'cause if I end up on your show, I'll be bound to her for years. Know what I mean?"

Phil nodded sympathetically.

"I know *exactly*. I had an agent like that, and to this day, I'm still paying them. It sucks. Don't you worry." He put his arm around me and gave my shoulder an avuncular squeeze. "I'll just call you at home. OK?" He hugged me. "Good-bye for now. I really look forward to working with you." He smiled at me, his eyes crinkling sweetly.

I spent the rest of the day hanging out with Sam and some of the other guys on the show. From what I gathered, there seemed to be quite a bit of unrest at *SNL* because the "boys" were not getting along with one of the girls who'd recently been hired. The atmosphere was warlike. The girl in question was a terrifically talented comic who maintained that the vibe over at *SNL* was at best childish and at worst completely misogynistic. She frequently made negative comments to the press about the show's poorly written material and sexist energy, the ongoing grievance of *SNL* women during the pre-Fey years. Sam and the rest of the boys insisted it was her own fault; she was "bitter," they said, "angry" and ultimately self-sabotaging.

From time to time, I would zone out during their gripes about their castmate or their assorted scatological bits and marvel to myself about how uncomplicated they were. Just doggies that wanted a cuddle and a cookie. No challenges, no complications, no fuss, no muss. "You're fun," they told me repeatedly, and I certainly was, smiling and flirting, laughing at all their jokes, an Auntie Tom, gamely going along with their gags and, to their surprise and delight, even adding some quips of my own. I was reminded of my father, who, though he adored that I had a mouth on me—goaded and encouraged it, in fact—never for a moment would have tolerated that same mouth used in any way against him. Throughout my childhood, he enjoyed me as his pal, guffawing on cue at the hilarity of my in-your-face antics, my rants and cutting observations, but always cautioning that, lest I think otherwise, dear Dad was surely unique in his appreciation; not all men would be so amused.

"Men don't like brawds who break their balls" was the pithy explanation, the neat little wrap-up that concluded our most uproarious exchanges, and I would come to view my father's oft-repeated assertion as a benediction of sorts, delivered absently but nonetheless pointedly from the cozy comfort of his La-Z-Boy recliner while he watched sports on TV. For many years, the scene played out exactly the same: me yammering about this or that, my father laughing and egging me on, until the moment came when, before turning his attention back to the TV, he would pause to reflect on his cheeky daughter with her big mouth, doomed to a lonely life of ball breaking. Our laughter would wane, turning soon to slow, irregular chuckles, until all that was left after a few audible sighs was the din of whistles and cheers and fans in stadiums beneath overcast skies.

Sitting in Sam's *SNL* dressing room that day, I hovered betwixt a sense of smug satisfaction that they all seemed to feel their balls were safe with me and, at the same time, exhaustion, as though I were carrying a building's worth of disloyalty to my gender.

And as the yukking it up reached a fever pitch, I psychically floated down the hall to the Angry Girl's dressing room and tried to imagine what it looked like inside.

At some point that afternoon, one of the boys got the idea to run up and tell Lorne Michaels that there was a chick there whom they actually *liked*, and by the way, she did a smokin' impersonation of Debra Winger. Before I left that day, I had a meeting set up for that Monday with Dan, *SNL*'s head talent coordinator.

By Sunday, I was in a full-blown panic. "This is insane—what will I even *do*?" I freaked out over the phone to Sam. "They're gonna want to see an *act*! I don't have an *act*! I'm not a comic; I only really have this ONE impersonation!"

"Aw, Goof, just go in and do the fuckin' Winger thing. We'll figure the rest out later . . ."

I went in for the Monday meeting and, after five minutes of pleasantries, did the bit from *An Officer and a Gentleman*, and Dan promptly opened up the big, black desk calendar. "I'd like you to meet Lorne," he announced. "How's Thursday?"

I was instructed to show up at midnight.

"Midnight?" I asked.

Dan nodded. "The meeting," he explained, "will actually be at one A.M., but it'd be good if you show up at midnight to get settled."

"Well, I'm not letting you loiter there by yourself," Billy whispered as we sat backstage on the closing night of the Molière play. "Robin and I will take you there, and we'll wait in the Rainbow Room. We'll toast you and take in the lovely view."

When I arrived at the studio, Dan escorted me to the Writers' Room, which was adjacent to Lorne's office. Sam and some of the other guys in the cast were there, and I was introduced to Al Franken, Norm MacDonald, and Tim, the director of *SNL*. As we sat around a conference table, Al, Norm, and Tim counseled me for over an hour on "How to Behave in Front of Lorne":

"Don't talk until he talks to you first!"

"Don't try to fill the silence!"

"Don't try to be funny!"

They practiced with me, doing mock Lorne scenarios, preparing me like a witness for a murder trial, as one A.M. came and went.

Finally, at two fifteen, I was ushered into Lorne's Lair.

I sat in between Al and Tim on a couch, Dan sat in a chair

next to the door, and Lorne sat behind his desk, his head slack, with a depressed mien that suggested a party's-over weariness. He was wearing sunglasses. Beside him was an assistant with a notepad and a pen, poised at the ready. There was silence for several long minutes while Lorne sat, staring at the floor. I started to wonder if he was napping. Finally, he looked in my direction.

"How long have you been doing stand-up?"

"I don't do stand-up, actually. I'm an actor."

Everyone shifted, cleared their throats, then more silence.

"What are you doing now?"

"Well, I just closed in this Molière play off-Broadway, and I'm about to start rehearsals for a downtown production of *Troilus and Cressida,* which is, you know, Shakespeare . . ."

I felt the air leave the room, as everyone's energy died in a glue trap of shared dread.

Lorne took off the shades and stared at me, wordless, for a while, then picked up a pen and pointed it at me, like an offering of some sort.

"I hear you do a good Debra Winger impersonation."

"Yes . . ."

"Can I see it?"

"Sure."

I stood up and did *An Officer and a Gentleman.*

Lorne was laughing pretty much all through it. His laugh was a sort of closed-mouth chuckle, which made him red in the face.

"Good," he pronounced, to everyone's relief. "Funny."

"She does other people, too, Lorne," Dan offered.

"So," Lorne declared ruminatively, "she does impressions and the like, but she's not a comic per se."

"Right," someone said. "But she was on *Remote Control,* and she wrote characters and stuff."

"Do you watch *SNL*?" Lorne asked me.

"Yeah," I lied. I'd maybe seen half an episode here or there, but the truth was, I hadn't watched it in years. "I've been watching it since it first came on the air; I grew up with it."

Lorne seemed to dig hearing that.

"What did you like about it? What's different, do you think, about it now?"

A few seconds went by as I thought about how the difference to me was that it used to be *good* and now it *sucked*.

Again the tension in the room seemed to mount.

"Well, you know, I think the thing was that . . . in the old days . . . there were these, you know . . . *characters* that . . . that were really, really popular, and the audience looked forward to seeing them every week. Like, they got excited if the Greek Diner or, you know, Roseanne Roseannadanna was on, or Belushi as the Samurai or, you know, whatever, and I think people might really miss that. And the *writing*, too. That was key, I think. All those sketches back then—well, they were *scenes*, really—were so well constructed, know what I mean? Really well-written *scenes*, really well-executed . . . beginnings, middles, and ends. I mean, look: the *writing* was just great. And then, of course, the *cast* was just so hilariously funny! And none of them stand-ups! They were just like these—obviously skilled improvisers—but ultimately they were just these really amazing comedic . . . *actors*. You know? Anyway, I think it would be great to maybe, you know . . . to somehow include those old elements again, back in the show."

Lorne nodded.

"Have you ever considered being blond?"

"Blond?"

"Yeah . . ." Lorne tilted his head and studied me.

"Well, sure," I said, trying to figure out where this was going. "Hasn't everyone?"

This elicited more laughter and mirth all around as everyone got to take part in imagining a revamped, better-looking me.

"Why? Do you think I'd look better as a blond or something?"

Lorne, like Louie Mayer on quaaludes, gazed groggily at me.

"Possibly," he nodded presciently. "Very possibly . . ." His voice trailed off, and he seemed to lose his train of thought for a moment.

"I want to set up an audition for you," he said finally, leaning back in his chair and putting his shades on. "But I'm not sure how since you don't have an *act*. The boys seem to like you, and that's a plus, so we should figure out a way to see you in front of an audience." He gestured toward his assistant, who started writing furiously. "In the meantime, start working up some characters and all your impressions, and we'll . . . we'll be in touch to set up another meeting."

"OK, sounds great," I said, standing up. "Well, thank you very much. Nice meeting you . . ."

A week or so later, Dan, the talent coordinator, called me.

"Lorne wants to see you tonight. In his office."

"You mean—to audition?"

"No, no, just a meeting."

"Oh. OK. What time?"

"I don't know. Sometime tonight. Can you just be . . . ready?"

I was dressed by four P.M. and sat on my couch and waited. And smoked. And waited.

Finally, at around nine P.M., Dan called.

"Can you be here at one thirty?"

I arrived at one thirty and at two A.M. was shown into Lorne's office, where I found him behind his desk, staring at the floor again. I was starting to think he had narcolepsy. Finally, he looked up and motioned for me to sit.

"You know, I used to date Debra Winger." He smiled sheepishly. I was floored.

"*Really?* I . . . I had no idea." Was this good or bad?

"Uh-huh."

"When?" I asked, not really knowing what the hell to do.

"When?" He looked at me blankly.

"Did you date Debra Winger? Was it . . . during *An Officer and a Gentleman?*"

"No. Later . . ."

"*Terms of Endearment?*"

"Later . . ."

I was at a loss. "*Mike's Murder?*" We both laughed.

"Yeah, around then." Our laughter died away awkwardly, and we were once again sort of looking around the room silently. Thinking we had finally had a decent exchange, and not knowing what I was really doing there, I continued on my line of Winger questioning.

"So, is she nice . . . Debra?" Lorne considered this and smiled, remembering something.

"She's . . . she's very . . . yeah. She's nice and she's very sexy. Very strong, very . . . fiery. Says what's on her mind. Doesn't take shit from anyone. We had fun."

For the first time, I was seeing a side of him that seemed vaguely human. I noticed he had sort of sad brown eyes that drooped in that way I had always liked and found approachable. Or one of his eyes did, anyway.

We were, once again, enveloped by quiet. During this time, I considered Lorne's Canadian accent, which had, for some reason, previously eluded me. I had always had a thing for Canadians; they had always seemed to me such a peaceful folk, taking our draft dodgers in the sixties, humanely doling out health care, saying "eh" after all thoughts.

I thought of the Mounties with those hats, and Joni Mitchell and Neil Young.

In sixth grade, I did a school report on Canada. While I was certainly intrigued by things like their Parliament and Francophones, I was mostly obsessed with Margaret Trudeau, the hot wife of the prime minister, who had a scandalous lost weekend at Studio 54 in the late seventies. Grainy pictures of Margaret, resplendent in her *blouson*, splashed across the *New York Post*'s front page as she discoed the nights away, on a glittery bender with Mick Jagger and Bianca and Halston. "What fun she is," I thought, "all freewheeling and naughty, rocking her designer jeans and Candies with the Beautiful People."

I didn't tell Lorne any of this, though. We just sat through the silence, waiting out his fugue, listening to the muffled sounds of life outside his door.

And then, he invited me to Chicago.

"I have to go out there to see some people at Second City in a few weeks," he explained. "We'll have you come along, and we'll set something up for you to perform there. We'll arrange something, some way for you to do an act there, in front of a crowd, and, you know, see how you do. How does that sound?"

"HUH? IT SOUNDS INSANE IS HOW IT SOUNDS," the voice in my head screamed. "I LIVE IN *NEW YORK*! WHAT'S WITH CHICAGO? AND WHAT'S WITH THE DEEPLY BIZARRE MIDDLE-OF-THE-NIGHT MEETINGS ABOUT NOTHING? YOU'RE A TOTAL FREEEEEAAK!"

"It sounds great," I said, and then I got up, smiled, and thanked him for the meeting.

I walked out of Rockefeller Center at around three A.M. and decided to walk the forty-something blocks home so that I could think.

In those days, I had a recurring dream of being in the opening number of *Cats*: as we slunk about the junkyard set during the first few bars, I would suddenly be overcome with panic because I had no idea which cat I was. Wandering home that night, I thought of how I had always interpreted this as merely an anxiety dream, an "actor's nightmare." But in the midst of the Lorne Michaels meetings and the prospect of getting hired for *SNL*, I understood the dream's divinatory significance: *I wasn't sure what kind of cat I was.*

I wanted a career as a working actor in the theater, to be involved in projects that meant something to me, plays I could feel proud of—but was I just kidding myself? Was I, in fact, really a "comedy chick"? Maybe. And maybe Lorne Michaels had the ideal job for me. Deep down, though, I hated the idea of it. I couldn't help thinking that even if hired, I would wallow, like I had over at *Remote Control*, where, when push came to shove, I could neither push nor shove, essential ingredients for thriving in comedy. Like *Remote*, *SNL* seemed to me like nothing more than a dead end. A dead end with endless late nights, embarrassing material, and bullies.

*Men don't like brawds who break their balls.*

*Saturday Night Live* seemed to me to be a sort of way station at which comics would bide their time, plotting how to turn characters that could barely sustain a sketch into big-budget movies. They wanted fame, and this was their conduit. But I didn't have any interest in being famous. Or did I? *Which cat am I?*

*The boys seem to like you, and that's a plus.*

I thought of my conversation the day before with my father.

"Don't blow this. Don't screw this one up," he had implored

me. "It's about time you stopped being such a goddamn snob about TV. Jesus! You used to love TV till that Mamet character got his meat hooks in. One *farkakte* play after the next. *What a waste!* You used to sing, you used to dance—*you were an entertainer, for Christ's sake!* Now, well . . . I dunno how you live with yourself, doin' all this crap. So, whatever you do, *don't screw this one up, I beg you!*"

The next week, rehearsals began for *Troilus and Cressida*. I was playing Helen of Troy, which, since she'd been abducted, was a very small part, so I spent most of my time in the dressing room, coming up with characters to put into an act I could do for Lorne. After rehearsals, I'd race over to my director friend Doug's apartment on Mott Street and try them out for him. We'd drink pitchers of iced coffee and smoke millions of cigarettes while I ran through everything over and over again, until finally, at dawn, I'd leave to get a few hours of sleep.

I heard from Dan, the *SNL* talent coordinator, that the Chicago trip was a go, but not for a few weeks. Since I had a week off from *Troilus and Cressida*, I decided to take a short trip to L.A. Billy's friend Robin suggested that she could "side-pocket" me under her big-shot agency's auspices for a while. I told her I was game, thrilled at the chance of escaping from Sandy, my malevolent troll agent, in her mother's Upper West Side apartment. Robin let me stay with her, and she set up a bunch of meetings. Various TV casting directors found me "likable" and were intrigued by my "heat" due to the *SNL* interest.

The best meeting by far was with the casting director of *Seinfeld*, who said that he felt sure there would be something for me to do on the show, and that if I lived in L.A., he'd bring me in to audition until I booked something.

"And, if you get some decent TV credits under your belt," Robin opined, "you'll definitely be able to book more stage work. Trust me."

I thought about what it might be like to live in L.A. It had never appealed to me before, but now, with the possibility of work, I felt differently. I felt seduced by the sun, the flatteries, and the attention. My friend Jane had moved out there a few years before and was always raving about how great it was. She was getting tons of TV jobs and buying expensive handbags without ever even looking at the prices. She told me that she would lie in the sun every day, reading scripts as she tanned. How bad could that be?

Looking ahead at the open road as I wove through the canyons, I experienced a peaceful resolve I hadn't felt in ages, as though the California expanse promised a surfeit of miracles. As I listened to eighties pop songs in my rented car, the lyrics that would normally have made me roll my eyes suddenly struck me as weighty and insightful. I wept listening to "Escape (The Pina Colada Song)," deeply moved that destiny had allowed the couple to find each other again.

I left L.A. feeling sun kissed, optimistic, and confused.

*Troilus and Cressida* opened to horrendous reviews a couple of weeks later, with one critic calling it "an embarrassment of embarrassments!"

Even my mother decided not to come.

Shortly after the show closed in May, I got a call from Dan at *SNL*, who said that the Chicago trip was scheduled for the following week.

"Lorne wants it to coincide with the Knicks-Bulls game he's going to with Bill Murray."

NBC sent me a round-trip business class ticket and told me I would be put up at the Ritz-Carlton, where Lorne and other

*SNL* staffers would also be staying. I was told there would be no per diem; for all food and drink, I'd be on my own.

I spent the next week polishing my makeshift act. The night before I left, I met Billy at our favorite haunt, Joe Allen's, for a drink.

"Well, darling, break a leg," he said, raising a glass of the cheap white wine he called Penis Grigio. "Things are going to change for you now. Forever . . ."

The next day, I arrived in Chicago around noon. While I was unpacking my things, I received a call from Dan, who told me that he and his assistant would take me over to Second City so I could get acclimated with the space where I'd be performing.

"Will I be going on tomorrow?" I asked in the cab on the way over.

"Yes," Dan said, nodding vigorously. "I really think so."

At the theater, we just sort of stood around for a couple of hours, schmoozing the Second City folks. I poked around a bit, asking about the itinerary for the weekend, but couldn't get any concrete answers. By the time I returned to my hotel room, I realized I was starving. I had been so nervous about everything, I'd forgotten to eat, so I picked up the menu and ordered the cheapest thing I could find, a sixteen-dollar chicken club sandwich with potato chips. As soon as I got off the phone with room service, Dan called.

"Lorne wants to meet with you later."

"OK . . ."

"He may want to see a few things, you know, as a preliminary . . ."

"You mean . . . wait—what do you mean? Like, I'd do some of . . . what I'm supposed to do for my audition?"

"Yeah. Sort of."

I thought it was weird, but what hadn't been weird?

"OK, um . . . what time?" I said, trying not to sound rattled. My audition now seemed to have a pre-audition.

"Not sure. I'll call you. Just—just stay put, OK?"

As I waited for my sandwich, I went over the notes for my act. When room service arrived, I flipped on the TV to watch while I ate, only to discover that Jacqueline Kennedy Onassis had died the night before. For the next few hours, I watched repeated press coverage of the outside of Jackie's Fifth Avenue apartment, interspersed with footage of her as First Lady, JFK's funeral, and scenic shots of Greece in the seventies.

"Wow," I thought. "She's really gone. *Jackie, Oh!*" I remembered how when I was fifteen my dad told me he had always loved her—until she married Aristotle Onassis.

"She *sullied* herself, you wanna know the truth," he instructed, late one night, as he devoured jumbo shrimps from a freezer storage bag over the kitchen sink. "She married that ugly Greek asshole—Christ, what a *meeskite* he was."

Watching Jackie clips in Chicago that night, I wondered which Jackie was the real Jackie: the sixties, Kennedy, Oleg-Cassini-muffs-and-hair-coiffed-within-an-inch-of-its-life Jackie or the seventies, windblown, capri-pants-Gucci-bag-and-ginormous-black-sunglasses Jackie? In theory, I agreed with my dad that Ari wasn't the greatest-looking guy, but I couldn't help thinking that Jackie was more herself—whatever that was—when she was with him and even later, after he died. Or maybe I wanted to believe that because the seventies Jackie was *my* Jackie—a Jackie I could get into. I loved the jet-set Jackie. The Jackie who hung out with Truman Capote and Misha Baryshnikov. The Jackie who chain-smoked and rode bikes braless with John-John in Central Park. The Jackie who got a gig at Doubleday even though she didn't need the cash. This was the sisters-are-doing-it-for-themselves Jackie, and now she was gone.

At eleven thirty, Dan called.

"So, Lorne's thinking maybe in an hour or so, you could come by his room?"

"OK. Does he want me to come at a certain time or—"

"No, no . . . I'll call you back. Just—stay put and I'll call you back."

I waited, watching more Jackie coverage. I was exhausted, so I ordered some coffee. At two thirty in the morning, the phone rang.

"Hi, Nancy. Dan, here . . . uh, listen, so I think tonight's a no-go. I'll call you in the morning, 'kay? You good?"

"Well, is—am I meeting with Lorne in the morning?"

"Yeah."

"And will this be . . . but, aren't I performing at Second City tomorrow night? I'm sort of not getting what the deal is. What time should I be up and ready by?"

"You're definitely performing tomorrow night, and, uh, Lorne wants to see you at some point tomorrow in the morning. I don't know what time yet, so just hang out in your room, and I'll call you, 'kay?"

I was flustered, but it was too late to call anyone. After a while, I fell into a fitful night's sleep, only to wake at seven A.M. in a panic. I took a shower, blew-dry my hair, got dressed, and put on makeup. Then I waited. And waited. At noon, Dan called.

"Hi. So, Lorne wants to get together with you, but he's trying to figure out his day, so things are still a bit murky. Can you hang out?"

"Yeah, I can, but for how long? And what time is the thing tonight?"

"I'm . . . yeah, I—I don't know—"

"Look, I'm not trying to be a pain, but Dan, I mean . . . I'm just sitting here—"

"I know, I know, and I'm really sorry. It's . . . I know, I know, I totally know. I'll call you back. Just hang. It'll be soon."

I couldn't leave. I guess I could have, but "soon" might have been any minute, and I didn't want to be unprofessional. As the day dragged on, I started to feel like Susan Hayward in *I Want to Live!*, waiting in jail watching the phone outside her cell, jumping at every terrifying jangle.

Hour after hour after hour passed. I watched Jackie getting married to Ari; watched her at the 1960 inaugural ball; watched her get off of Air Force One in her bloody pill box getup. I called Dan once out of desperation, but there was no answer in his room. At six, I received a call from Lorne's assistant informing me that there was a "change of venue" and Second City wasn't going to work. Someone would be in touch within the hour to give me an address.

I was starving. I hadn't eaten all day, so I ordered another chicken club sandwich with potato chips. Fuck it, I figured, and turned up the volume to watch an early-sixties televised special of Jackie taking the American people through a tour of the White House after her renovations.

I sat eating my sixteen-dollar sandwich, marveling at how breathy Jackie's voice was. Did she really talk that way? Was that her real voice, or was that some kind of polite lady way of speaking back then? She sounded like she wanted to make herself as ethereal as possible, as if having any bottom to her voice would make her gauche and unappealing. It was as though she was attempting to be invisible, which was how I felt sitting aimlessly in another city eating potato chips on an unmade hotel bed.

My friend Kevin, a soap actor who lived in L.A., called to see how it was going.

"Are you fucking kidding me?" he asked, incredulously. "*Get outta there!* Just take off, man. Let them find you! Go see a movie! Go buy some shit in the Water Tower and have dinner. Fuck 'em. Lemme tell ya: they all just wanna make money and *be blown*, and they don't give a flying fuck about the actors, man. I say you just split; get outta the room and go cruise Chi-Town."

I wanted to do what he was telling me, but I couldn't. I was too afraid.

At eight thirty, I got a call from Lorne's assistant.

"Hi, Nancy, OK, it'll be any minute now."

"What's gonna be any minute?"

"Oh—didn't Dan talk to you?"

"No."

"Oh, uh, OK—lemme call you back."

"Wait! What's going on? Am I seeing Lorne? And where's Dan?"

"He's . . . wait—you know what, I'll have Dan call you, OK? He'll call you in ten minutes."

I called Robin in L.A.

"I'm seriously going out of my mind. What should I do? I've been holed up here since yesterday! It's almost nine at night!"

There was a knock at my door.

"This might be them! This might be it—I'll call you back."

Click.

I answered the door. It was housekeeping. Did I want turn-down service? Suddenly, standing there with the maid and her cart in my doorway, I realized that this wasn't going to happen. There would be no audition. I would leave Chicago the next morning, having accomplished nothing. Except for maybe becoming an authority on Jackie Kennedy.

I flipped on the TV, and there she was again, giving her first post-assassination sit-down interview. The phone rang.

"Hi, Nancy." It was Lorne's assistant. "So . . . ugh, I'm really so, so sorry. Tonight's just not good, and in a way, this is better for you, 'cause Lorne's actually in a bit of a bad mood because the Knicks lost, and he's just . . . he's just not in a *good space* right now, you know?"

"Uh-huh." I turned up the volume on the TV. It was Richard Burton singing "Camelot." "So. OK. Is that it?"

"Yeah. I'm—I'm real sorry that this has all been so, like, you know . . ."

"*In Camelot! Camelot!*" Burton's voice boomed in the background.

"But it's really better for you this way, and you can get the benefit of Lorne seeing you when he's, you know, in a better, like, space."

"*In Camelot! Camelot!*"

"So, um . . ." the assistant continued, "Dan will, uh, call you to set up another . . . something for you to, um, you know—another time. 'Kay?"

I sat on my bed and lit a cigarette, feeling too spent to cry. I ordered another chicken club sandwich with potato chips and ate it while I watched Sarah Michelle Gellar in a made-for-TV movie called *A Woman Named Jackie*. At around midnight, I drifted off to sleep.

The next morning, as I was leaving the hotel to catch my flight back to New York, I ran into Dan in the hallway. I was wearing sunglasses. My mother had always told me that if you're wearing sunglasses and you run into someone you know, you should flip them up; it's rude not to let your acquaintance see your eyes. I kept my shades down, like Jackie O, covering my eyes. I was done being polite. And, I was done being Winger.

"I'm so sorry, Nancy," Dan began. "But we'll *definitely* be getting you in—"

"You realize that I was trapped, right? You guys kept telling me that this thing would be any minute now, and I was trapped in my room for two days, eating expensive sandwiches."

"You know what?" he said gallantly. "Get me your bills—get me your receipts and we'll take care of it. For sure. OK? And I'll call you—*really soon*—to set up a—a *situation* for you to do your thing. OK?"

I walked into the elevator and didn't look back. On the trip home, I made a decision: I would tell Lorne, Dan, Tim, and the various assistants to go fuck themselves; I would move to Los Angeles and buy into the myth that TV credits could be parlayed into a life on the stage. I figured I would hit that scene now, while I had some casting people interested.

I had Robin call Dan at *SNL* to tell him that I was "no longer interested" and "moving to L.A."

In the ensuing weeks, when people heard the *SNL* story, I was heralded as a hero by some people and derided as a fool by others. An agent I knew at the William Morris Agency who'd been intensely following the *SNL* activity said, "You're out of your fucking mind," and told me that I should "go back there, to 30 Rock, right now, crawling on your hands and knees, *apologize,* and *beg* Lorne to give you another chance!"

I never heard back from Phil Hartman; plans for his variety show were scrapped and NBC instead folded him into their new sitcom *NewsRadio*.

The night I arrived back home from Chicago, I went to Billy and Bobby's for dinner.

"Nancele's here," Billy announced, greeting me at the door with a tumbler of vodka. "She's going to tell us about those cunts at *Saturday Night Live*—"

"WHOOOOOO'S A CUNT?" Bobby yelled out from his bedroom.

"The people at *Saturday Night Live*—"

"THEY CALLED HER A 'CUNT'?" Bobby stood astonished in the doorway.

"No," Billy said, laughing. "*They're* cunts. They made her go to Chicago for nothing."

"Well, baby," Bobby laughed, taking a sip of vodka. "That's television."

Three months later, I flew to Los Angeles for good. It was right about the time that Debra Winger left show business and re-treated to the East Coast, and I sometimes wonder if, high above the clouds, our paths crossed. I never impersonated her again.

## 5. The Stuff That Dreams Are Made Of

**I scored the** first job I auditioned for when I got to Los Angeles, playing a jailed biker on a doomed sitcom that was a vehicle for some comic. I had been in town less than twenty-four hours, having arrived at the sparsely furnished Hollywood Hills bachelor pad I would be house-sitting, along with an amiable actor named Jeff, late in the afternoon the day before. I was thrilled; I had hit the ground running. A few auditions later, I landed a role on *Seinfeld*.

"I wanna tell you something," my father said when I called to share my big news. "You are a very courageous person. I've always said it. You are a person of great courage." He continued to wax emotional for a while, and I sat on the floor, listening and nodding, so happy I could make my father proud. I was always seeking such moments, clinging to them feverishly when they arrived, never fully embracing an accomplishment unless it had been acknowledged and appreciated by him first. I suppose most people seek out parental approval, but I often think that a performer's thirst for this praise is even more heightened— perhaps unquenchable. I always felt that the single most amazing revelation about Madonna in the "rockumentary" *Truth or Dare* (aside from the nonpareil virtuosity she exhibited deepthroating a Perrier bottle) was how desperate she was to please her dad. And how could anyone not relate to that? After making my father sit through years of theater he neither understood nor enjoyed (on uncomfortable chairs), I was finally doing something he could get behind: a part on a hit network television show that everyone he knew watched. I could picture him: watching me on the tube, kvelling, lying in his black leather recliner receiving phone calls from his friends, other lawyers dotted around the country, all duly impressed. The whole thing did feel rather lionhearted all of a sudden. Before decamping to Hollywood, I had decided that getting a gig on *Seinfeld* would be my litmus test: if I was hired, it would be a harbinger of impending success. I don't know why; I had never even watched the show. But I knew everyone else did, and in an uncharacteristically bold way, this is what I set my sights on.

After I hung up with my father, I lay on the floor daydreaming about my soon-to-be-swelling bank account and what I'd say to Oprah when she asked me if I "always knew this was my destiny." "Yes," I'd say as the camera panned into an audience of solicitous Midwesterners. "Yes, I did." Later that night, watching myself in the steamy mirror of my Advanced Spinning Class, I continued to marvel at my streak of providence: "I *am* doing the right thing," I mused while frantically pedaling on a sawed-off bike, going nowhere. "These things are happening for me because I am doing the *right thing*."

Booking this job was a major coup, particularly because my first *Seinfeld* audition was a disaster. When I visited L.A. in the midst of the Lorne Michaels craziness, Robin sent me to meet the *Seinfeld* casting director, a very nice guy with whom I immediately hit it off. He called me back that afternoon to meet with the producers, and I sat anxiously in a fluorescently lit waiting area, watching girls teetering in and out of "the Room," all of them wearing skimpy skirts and tight little tees. I looked down at my drab, shapeless, black New York Actor rehearsal getup, which was fine if I was auditioning for a deconstructed version of *King Lear* on Ludlow Street, and thought nervously, "They'll get it—right?"

The Room was crammed with at least twenty Jewish guys and one lone woman (the writers and producers), not to mention the director, Larry David, and Jerry Himself. I was so intimidated I didn't even *look at them* when I was introduced, keeping my gaze instead on the casting director, who read the scene with me. Absolutely petrified, I couldn't breathe, and I shook like I suffered from Parkinson's. My voice never got louder than a weird, raspy whisper. Worse, I didn't look up from my script on the punch line. Oh my god. If there is anything you do on a sitcom audition, no matter what, ALWAYS, for god's sake, LOOK UP ON THE JOKE. Even if the script is the worst, most unfunny thing you've ever read in your life (usually it is!), look up on the joke. I've landed jobs where I'd taken only the most cursory glance at the script before the audition, merely because I made sure I looked up on the joke.

When it was over, someone halfheartedly muttered, "Thank you," whereupon I slunk away, like a dog that's been reprimanded for peeing on the carpet. Driving back through Coldwater Canyon in a daze, I thought about my friend Jane, now starring in something like her eighth pilot. What had she told me about the importance of auditioning with good hair?

*Always get your hair blown out—you'll feel stronger.*

*Of course it's important to be funny, but it's more important to look sexy.*

I pictured her, a plethora of firm convictions and beauty products, sitting on my couch and delivering wise nuggets while I stomped around screaming about feminism and art. Even the Jazz Musician, ever the artiste, told me that when hiring a "chick singer," the "cats" in the band ask themselves two questions: (1) What does she look like? And (2) can she sing? Weaving through the canyon, I had a Helen Keller "wah-wah" moment: I had gone about it all wrong, preparing for the audition by *working on the script*. But I wasn't actually *prepared*—not outwardly.

Strangely, the casting director didn't attribute the hideousness of that audition to me and told Robin that the "energy in the room was off"; they (meaning Jerry) were just "having a bad day." He assured her that he would bring me in again. That was March. Six months later, at the end of September, Robin called: I was getting another chance. I told myself I wasn't going to make the same mistakes this time. There was no way I was going back into the Room without confidence. No more baggy clothes, no more hair in my face, no more "don't look at me, I'm just this cool, unassuming, artsy chick." I decided to take a few of Jane's tips. I went to a hot new place called Estilo—Spanish for "style"—to have my hair professionally blown out. Then I did something I'd never done before: I stuffed. Jane had long ago suggested that I use "chicken cutlets" to augment my boobs, and I didn't really know what she meant. But a few hours before the audition, I was at Neiman Marcus buying new underwear and I saw them: silicone inserts that looked like six-pound boneless, skinless kosher chicken breasts, ready to be stuffed into your Wonderbra. They were expensive—a hundred dollars—and I was pretty broke, but I was mesmerized. I couldn't walk away. It was like stumbling onto the Rosetta Stone and then saying, "But how will I get it back? I have so much luggage already." Whipping out my plastic, I charged a pair, dashed home to Nichols Canyon, and locked myself in the bathroom. With my hair bouncin' and behavin' and my "TV-ready" makeup emphasizing my pouty lips, I stuffed the cutlets in, pulled down my tight, low-cut T-shirt, and took a gander at myself in the bathroom mirror from the side. "Jesus. I look good with tits," I thought. I felt a twinge of guilt about it, but . . . "It makes sense for me to have tits," I decided. On my way out, I found Jeff eating a taco in the kitchen.

"Well," I said, grabbing my keys, "I'm finally getting another shot at *Seinfeld*. What d'ya think?"

"Wow," he said, his eyes popping out, his mouth full of food. "Nice ta-tas!"

"I know—right?"

"Where'd you get those?"

"Neiman Marcus!"

"Awesome!"


"That was *wonderful*!" Jerry enthused after I finished my reading. I turned to face the sea of beaming, ebullient faces. I smiled sweetly, chirped, "Thank you! Byeee!," waved, and practically skipped out of the room. I sailed back over the hill, singing "Tits and Ass" from *A Chorus Line* the whole way, and by the time I got home, there was a message on the voice mail from Robin telling me I'd gotten the part.

I arrived an hour early for my first day of rehearsal, went to grab some coffee and a bagel ("Jerry has them shipped in from New York," the first AD told me. "He *loathes* L.A. bagels"), and encountered Jerry, scarfing down a bowl of cereal. Like his character on the show, Jerry was always with the cereal.

"Well, there she is!" he exclaimed enthusiastically, extending his hand out as though presenting me. "The girl with the hair in her face! Nice to see you, Nancy! Welcome!"

"Hey, Jerry," I said. "Thanks for having me on!"

Even with the expensive blowout, my hair still managed to

droop into my face. Ned, when he was my teacher, was constantly harping about my hair being in my face during scene work.

"Nance," he'd say, shaking his head, "what's with the hair? What are you trying to hide? Get it the fuck off your face. Next time, I won't let you even start the scene without barrettes."

I snapped to just as the makeup and hair people rushed over to get a look at me.

"Keep her hair natural looking," Jerry warned them as they swarmed around me wielding measuring tape, notepads, and concerned expressions.

"No big hair—and make sure it's off her face," he smiled at me, then hopped on his skateboard and zoomed off, leaving them to their appraisals. In the end, they made me look great, and I even went to the Christophe Salon in Beverly Hills, where there was a very snobby lady with a fake-sounding French accent who ran the front desk (I was sure she was really from Queens), and got my hair highlighted for the first time. I had never felt so pretty. I loved the new me, even if she was a lot of smoke and mirrors and peroxide and rubber.

Rehearsals went remarkably smoothly the whole week. The episode's baroque plot is built around the premise that Jason Alexander's character, George, believes he has unwittingly purchased the actor Jon Voight's old Chrysler LeBaron. Jon Voight, in a cameo, played himself; I played a dental hygienist named Terry, who gets cruised by Kramer at Tim the Dentist's Thanksgiving party. I was treated royally by everyone on the show. They were some of the nicest people I've ever worked with, warm and generous, and the vibe on the set was totally relaxed and fun.

Once, when the air-conditioning in my trailer broke, Jerry came out to have a look. "Here, hold this," he said, handing me his turkey sandwich and standing on a chair. He stood there, jiggling something in the ceiling, and voilà: he fixed it.

Who knew?

On the day of the taping, Michael Richards invited me to join them for a preshow catered Chinese meal on the set, but I was so nervous I couldn't eat. The taping, which took something like three hours, flew by. The klieg lights came on, we were rolling, the laughs came as planned. Jerry announced my name and brought me out for my curtain call with the cast. It was thrilling. After my scene wrapped, Larry David gave me a hug. "You did it!" he said, and I breathed a sigh of relief before practically floating home around midnight.

For the next month, I stayed busy doing voice-overs and auditioning. I got my hair blown out before everything and started keeping the chicken cutlets in the trunk of my car—along with extra head shots and résumés—in case I had to whip them out for any last-minute auditions. Casting people were invariably impressed that I had just worked on *Seinfeld*, and I had to regale them with what it was like to work there and details of the episode's nutty plotline. One slightly disappointing side note was that people were always asking me what Jon Voight was like, and I had to say I had no idea. His one scene was shot ahead of time, so he hadn't been at the taping.

The episode aired during November Sweeps, when networks stack their decks with celebrity guest stars, hoping to garner immense ratings and wipe their asses with their network opponents. Commercials for the episode ran ad nauseam, and for the entire week prior to its airing, I got calls from people I hadn't talked to in years who had seen flashes of me saying my big laugh line: "Wait—Jon Voight bit you?," with the funky *Seinfeld* bass riffs playing in the background. I was ridiculously excited.

The day the show aired, I spoke to my father in the morning.

"I've got about a hundred people watching tonight," he gushed. "Everyone's really excited!"

"That's great," I said, feeling butterflies in my stomach for the first time.

"I wanna call you right after—you gonna be home?"

Because my parents were on the East Coast, they would be seeing the show three hours earlier than me. At six thirty that night my time, I sat next to the phone and waited. And waited. Where was he? Maybe he was fielding phone calls from friends? Finally, at five past seven the phone rang. It was my mother.

"Hi—" she said, though it sounded more like a "huh," like she was being slapped on the back during a chest exam.

"Hi . . ." I volleyed back, after which followed a protracted pause.

"Sooooo!" she intoned. Was she hoping I would think that was a sentence?

"Did you watch it?" I asked finally.

"Yes . . ."

"And?"

"It was good. It was . . . *short*."

"Short?"

"Yes. But it was very good."

"Where's Daddy?"

"He's—he's . . ." Her voice trailed off.

"Yeah?"

"He's asleep. He has to get up early tomorrow."

What happened to I was so courageous, I was a hero, *yadda, yadda, yadda*?

I don't know how long I sat in the darkened living room of that seventies-style ranch house, staring at the enormous turned-off television set. I don't recall what I thought about either. I remember at one point getting up and walking around and around the Ping-Pong table—the only other piece of furniture besides the TV and a frayed club chair—before perching on it and staring out the glass sliding doors into the dusky canyon. Jeff came home with chips and beer in time to watch me in a part that had been cut so significantly that if you blinked, you missed me. And then there was my hair. Once again, my hair, the subject of so much conversation and concern, almost completely obscured my face.

"But the highlights look great," Jeff offered. "They really look great on camera, and so did you."

"Do you think they cut me 'cause I sucked?"

"Probably not. It's just what happens on sitcoms. Happens all the time: they always cut stuff from guest spots and costars; if it's not having to do with the regulars, they figure it's extraneous. Don't worry, there'll be other gigs."

And there were. Even on *Seinfeld*, where three years later I appeared again, in two episodes of the ninth and final season. By that time, I had figured out I needed to grow out my bangs, as well as the advantages of Final Net. I wish I felt proud or even just happy about being a footnote on one of the most successful shows in the history of television, but I don't. Whenever it's mentioned, I feel the same emptiness that I did sitting on that crummy Ping-Pong table in Nichols Canyon.

My father and I never spoke about it again. It became one of those verboten subjects, glossed over, ignored, as if it had never happened in the first place. My mother told me that sometime after the episode aired, they ran into a lawyer they knew in a hotel elevator, whose actor son had become a big star. My father congratulated her for her son's success; she thanked him, saying, "Yes, we are very proud." The woman then asked, "Isn't your daughter in the business too?" Apparently, my father could only nod and glumly look down at the floor. "It was so hard for him," my mother said. And I'm sure it was.

I would later find, in a box in my parents' bedroom, a series of fuzzy pictures, four frozen frames of me in the Jon Voight episode. Two were of me, Jason Alexander, and Michael Richards; one was of me in close-up with my hair in my face; and one was of my name in the closing credits. It appeared that someone had first videotaped the episode, then snapped a photo of each of these frames. I have since wondered if the photos were my father's handiwork, or perhaps an offering from some cousin on Long Island for whom those faint glimpses of a family member on television were worthy of a craft project.

As for the rubber tits: one day, on the Disney lot, in the depths of the San Fernando Valley, I pulled them out of the car trunk, where they lay dormant and roasting. The burning silicone actually scalded my finger. I went in for the appointment titless and got a callback, so I never used them again. Years later, when I was moving from one apartment to another, I came across one of them, its mate nowhere to be found. I couldn't bring myself to throw it away, but I couldn't take it with me either, so I wrapped it in Saran Wrap and left it in the fridge.

# 6. More Mud: Mud Season (Reprise)

**After four months** of house-sitting in Nichols Canyon, I moved to my second home in Los Angeles, also in the Hollywood Hills, a section loftily known as Hollywood Heights. My agent, Robin, had finessed an apartment swap with another of her clients, whereby the client would take my place in New York, I would take hers, and then we'd reassess. We agreed on a six-month commitment, which was about all I could wrap my mind around at that point.

I went one gray afternoon in early December to have a look at the place: a teensy basement apartment in a charming, ramshackle cottage built in the 1920s, overgrown with gnarly vines of night-blooming jasmine and sheltered by a huge wisteria tree. When I arrived, someone was listening to the original Broadway sound track of *Company*, and as I parked the car, I could hear Elaine Stritch bellowing "The Ladies Who Lunch." A tall, boyishly handsome guy of about forty with sky blue eyes and a sly grin greeted me at the door. It was Jimmie, my apartment swapper's best friend, who rented the upstairs part of the cottage with his wife, Mary, and their two young daughters.

"Well, I know I'm in the right place if you're playing Stritch," I told Jimmie, and he laughed.

"Stritch is *heaven*," he said, shaking his head. "Absolute *heaven*."

After Jimmie showed me around, I decided the place would be fine. I went back to New York to collect my cat, Max, who'd been staying for a few months with a friend, and returned to my new home in early January in the midst of a raging storm that locals quaintly called El Niño, Spanish for "little boy." I quickly discovered that the heating was faulty and the bedroom flooded. Mold flourished in various areas of the soggy wall-to-wall carpet, and the bedsheets were musty and dank. I poured Max—still strung out on kitty dope—out of his bag and took in the scene. My first gander at this place had been so fleeting, it felt like I was only just then seeing it for the first time. Known as a "mother-in-law apartment," it was configured like a railroad flat: rooms spilling into each other, with the kitchen at one end, the bedroom at the other, and the dining area, bathroom, and living room floating betwixt the two. From the bedroom window, there was a view down the hill of the Hollywood Holiday Inn, whose green neon letters I could still make out through the fog.

Heavy, dark furniture of some forgotten era was wedged into every corner, dwarfing the space and accentuating the freakishly low ceiling. It was like a cheap, dilapidated dollhouse saved from a roadside tag sale. There was a great deal of mismatched china housed in a whitewashed Shabby Chic–style cabinet, some of it chipped and junky, some of it fancy, as though the person to whom it belonged had over the years fallen in and out of hard times, hocking the good stuff now and again, or perhaps just losing things with every unforeseen hasty move. In the living room, a sad sofa, some kind of Jennifer Convertible on its last gasp, smelling vaguely of bergamot, mildew, and ylang-ylang, was outfitted with scarfy crushed-velvet fabrics and various silk shawls, giving it a Stevie Nicks *Tusk* Tour vibe. I sat on it with Max that first afternoon, listening to the pelting rain, dispirited and shivering, reading yellowed aromatherapy books until dark.

The next morning, following a brief respite from the downpour, I went out in my rented Nissan to pick up groceries. Pulling into the perilously sloped driveway, I yanked up the emergency brake and started to grab my stuff, then heard a tap on my window. It was Ned.

"Well, howdy, neighbor," Ned grinned, hands stuffed in his pockets. I hadn't seen him in two years, since we'd been caught on another coast, in another driveway, frantically trying to escape the mud. He had tried to reach me many times after that ill-fated trip—sending me cards, letters, chocolates—but I'd blown off these attempts until eventually he'd stopped.

"Ned! What are you doing here?" I said, hugging him a bit tentatively.

"I live here! Two houses up! Renting a real sweet little guesthouse. All wood. Very Mission style, which, as you know, is my yen."

I couldn't get over the randomness, to say nothing of the awkwardness. Here we were in Los Angeles—huge, sprawling, colossally spread-out Los Angeles—on a *minor* hill, not a *major* Hollywood hill, mind you, but a teeny little offshoot hill of no import. And of all the neighbors on all of the hills in all of Los Angeles, who happens to be my two-doors-down neighbor?

Ned had been living in his rented guesthouse for a couple of months. He had run into Mary one day, who'd told him that an actress from New York was moving in—maybe he knew her?

"So I've been waiting for you to show up! Kept looking in the driveway to see if there was a new car—gosh—for at least a week now. Startin' to feel like a Peeping Tom . . . or a Peeping

Ned!" he blurted, laughing easily. Despite internal eye-rolling at his familiar corniness, I laughed too. Why not? The whole thing was just absurd.

"How've you been?" he asked.

*How had I been.* It was a simple question to which there was no simple answer. In the midst of this latest transition in my life, I was at once elated and forlorn. I was terribly lonely and frequently overwhelmed, but as much as I hated to admit it, I loved L.A. I loved driving; I loved the weather; I loved the smell of jasmine everywhere. As a person with absolutely no sense of direction, I felt like a genius in L.A. because I knew that if I was facing the hills, I could take a left and be at the beach sometime before the end of the day.

"Find the hills," my Nichols Canyon roommate Jeff would intone. "That's all you gotta do." Things like this made me feel like I was on track with everything else. New York agents and casting people had always maintained, "Oh, they'd never get you in L.A. Never!" Yet from the beginning, every time I went in for a meeting, Robin would call me up and shriek into her speakerphone, "IT WAS A LOVEFEST!" I was getting work, making money, stockpiling credits with which I hoped to transform my career—it was all happening.

And yet, I couldn't shake the insidious depression that clung to me like thick early-morning smog draped over the Santa Monica Mountains. Like Pigpen in Charlie Brown, my dark, dirty cloud preceded me and lingered when I left. There was no reason for it and every reason in the world. Along with the various successes of my first few months in L.A., there were some abysmal moments as well. Within weeks of my arrival in September, I fell back into bed with the Jazz Musician, who happened to be in L.A. for some gigs. I assured myself it was all

"fine." I could be *casual*; I lived in *Hollywood*; I was *working*;
I had *call times* and *trailers*. But the truth was I hoped we would
get back together, so when, at the end of our two-week sex bender, the Jazz Musician departed, I was once again devastated. If
it's "once burned, twice shy," then surely the third time around
is a metaphysical holocaust.

Then Robin announced that she was leaving her big Hollywood agency and moving to New York. She wanted a husband
and was convinced that unlike Los Angeles Jewish Men, who
were nothing but smarmy lookists, New York Jewish Men were
kindly and deep and didn't care if you had a big ass. She took a
job at a midlevel agency—a big step down from where she had
been—moved in with a gay guy, and waited for marriage pro-
posals that would never come. For a while, Robin and I continued to work together from opposite coasts, but casting people
started telling me I would need to get someone new in town if I
planned on staying. I was shattered. I had finally found a com-
passionate, interested agent who believed in me and got me auditions, and now she was gone. I signed with someone else, but
it wasn't the same. For all the exciting feats of the fall, I could
now only focus on my losses; while on the plane back to L.A.,
with my drugged cat in a bag under my seat, I listened over and
over to the plaintive strains of *Ladies of the Canyon* on my Dis-
cman, weeping disconsolately.

I didn't tell any of this to Ned, though. I told him I was fine,
and he said it was great to see me, and even though I probably
hated him, would I have lunch with him? I told him I didn't hate
him and without hesitation agreed to lunch. We ate at A Votre
Sante, a vegan place down on La Brea, and within minutes we
were once again "pals." Whatever weirdness might have been
lurking quickly evaporated; I easily forgot *why* Ned and I had

stopped speaking (again), and apparently, so did he. I knew he was sorry it had all gone the way it had, and in that moment I was too.

"Hey," he said as we tucked into our fake Chocolate Satin Pie. "I missed you. A whole lot."

I saw the earnestness in his watery green eyes. They were, as usual, rimmed with the faintest red—the by-product of his habitual Wake 'N Bake—making them even greener.

"I missed you too," I said, and I had.

"I won't lie to you and say I don't adore you and wouldn't be delighted to get down your pants, but if I say I'll behave, can we still be pals? I mean, we *are* neighbors."

I laughed. "And you might need to borrow a cup of sugar?"

He grinned. "If that's the only kind of sugar you're willing to put out, then, yeah!"

Ned, since last I had seen him, had clearly begun an ascent in his career, and yet he was still the same ol' Ned. He hadn't changed a bit and in that moment, it was a source of great comfort. When I looked across the table at him, I saw Ned, a person from my past, with whom I shared memories, some good, some not so good. But I also saw myself, the me Ned had taught, the me whom Ned had such enormous faith in, the kick-ass me I used to be, but of late had trouble not only accessing but even remembering. He was my past, but he also inspired my hopes for a future that, after many years of effort, could in the end work out: Ned had recently won the role of a lifetime, the role that would ultimately make him very rich and very famous.

"Finally, after all these years, I figured the whole fucking thing out," he told me as we finished our meal. "They were gonna pass me by, so I flew myself to New York—on my dime—auditioned for them again, and as I was leaving, I told them, point-blank, 'Don't make a mistake, fellas. I'm the guy.' "

The story didn't surprise me. Two years prior, right before the Maine Mud Fiasco, I accompanied Ned to the premiere of a movie in which he had a small, supporting role. Most of his part, however, ended up on the cutting room floor. Walking up to the after-party, we came to a press line. A few of the stars preceded us down the line, shutterbugs snapping away, flashes going off like the Fourth of July. But as soon as they had their shots of the stars, they stopped shooting, seeing Ned and me as an opportunity to reload. Ned stood there for a few seconds, waiting for them to take his picture.

"Ned," I whispered, "they're not gonna take our picture. We should just go in. Come on. We should keep walking . . ."

Ned was outraged.

"Fuck them," he fumed, grabbing my hand and storming up the press line, back where we had come from, furiously bumping into people.

"I'm not going to their stupid fucking party. Fuck them all. I am going to be a BIG, FAT, FUCKING MOVIE STAR. THAT'S IT! I've had it!" It was then that Ned focused his laser: he knew what he wanted, said it out loud—demanded it, even—and made it happen.

Even so, he seemed unchanged by the results. This was certainly a far cry from the other people I knew who had moved to L.A. from New York, a strange and remote, weirdly paranoid, and hard-to-reach group. Some people didn't resemble their former selves in the slightest; they were all new noses, new hair colors, new names, new personalities. People who had always been dramatic actresses were all of a sudden comedians; stand-up comics were playing it straight; playwrights were suddenly sitcom writers. A director I knew who claimed to have regularly partied with John-John Kennedy was now a Hasidic Jew. Pathological liars who had made crazy claims about Pacino and De

Niro were actually doing jobs with Pacino and De Niro. It was like that line in *My Man Godfrey*: "All you need to start an insane asylum is a room and the right kind of people." At that moment, I thought that Ned and I were the only two sane people in the whole Wild West. Little did I realize how much we fit in.

"I think this is a *sign*," my mother said ominously when I called to tell her the story later.

"Of what?"

"What do you *think*?" she asked superciliously. My mother was quite possibly the least spiritual person I had ever known. Yet in moments like this—when she wanted me to do something—she liked to adopt an enigmatic, otherworldly tone.

"That you should give this one a try," she continued. "You've never really *tried* with him. And now here he is, *literally, on your doorstep*. I think it's a great story."

"Sorry to ruin the 'great story,' but I don't think we really have that much actual chemistry. I mean as a couple."

"Oh, horseshit. You never really tried!"

"Plus, he's a complete weed freak . . ."

"So? No one's perfect!"

"He's a total sexist . . ."

"Oh, *please,* what man isn't? I mean, this guy is on the brink of some great things. He's goin' places. You really don't want to miss *that* boat!"

My mother was right about one thing: I hadn't tried. And as I sat on my sodden bed staring at the Hollywood Holiday Inn's neon sign, I tried to remember all the reasons why. I knew everything I needed to know about Ned and why the boat to which my mother referred was a sinking one, but nostalgia is a corrupting sentiment: you imagine half-truths; you resort to magical thinking.

In the weeks that followed, Ned and I spent a lot of time together, eating "healthy Chinese" at the Mandarette on Beverly, occasionally seeing movies, and, weather permitting, working on auditions on his back patio. We would drive down the boulevards at night in his convertible, with the top down and the heat blasting, laughing and arguing over various script analyses. I promptly forgot all about Ned's antediluvian attitudes, his potential for cruelty, his selfishness, his inability to listen to anything offstage, and his peerless penchant for pot, and one night, when he put the moves on me, I didn't even stop him. There was no sense asking myself what I was thinking; I wasn't thinking anything at all. It was very simple: I was lonely; Ned was lonely too. Ned still pined for Binky; I still pined for the Jazz Musician. We knew better, and yet for some reason, Ned and I, in our thirst for love, clung to each other, both hoping that what we already knew could somehow be unknown. While Ned set about trying to turn me into the girly-girl of his dreams by obsessively buying me, not lingerie from Victoria's Secret, but rather, long flannel nightgowns edged with lace that buttoned up the neck into Annie Sullivan–esque Victorian choke holds, I meanwhile tried to (a) overlook the fact that I had never, in my entire life, worn a nightgown and (b) convince myself that "growing into" passionate love was possible, even preferable. Perhaps then, I theorized, I wouldn't lose myself so entirely as I had done in the past, abnegating every last bit of my power, holding fast to the fiction of soul mates and true love. And how could I know if any of this was possible if I never tried?

*You don't want to miss that boat.*

"I'll jump aboard," I told myself, "then fling myself over the rails—flannel bondage nightie and all—if it all goes asunder."

In the end, though, it turned out not to matter what narrative I repeated to get myself going, because Ned couldn't get going at all: once given the green light, Ned couldn't get it up.

Well. Naturally, according to him, this was, without question, *my* fault; had I not been so difficult to lay all these years, he wouldn't have had any problems. All that prelude—not to mention the buildup—wasn't exactly fortifying to his masculinity. No guy, Ned insisted, would have been able to perform under such withering circumstances. Vowing repeatedly that this had never, ever happened to him before he was subjected to my humiliations and brazen withholding, he lay on the bed after the offending incident, prostrate with bewilderment, for several long minutes, unable to move, visions of the Interruptus loop de looping in his head. As I sprawled next to him, staring at the whirling ceiling fan, it occurred to me that I had finally arrived at the point in my life wherein the metaphorical had become the actual: I had literally broken a man's balls.

"I don't understand it," Ned remarked finally. "Binky and I used to fuck like rabbits, and it was always, *always* great."

That I continued to hang out with Ned—and he with me—after the various indictments spawned by our failed coitus attempt only proved beyond a shadow of a doubt that misery loves company, frigid hussies and flaccid cocks notwithstanding. The disappointment of this episode, however, must have caused a kind of short circuit in Ned's psyche, because the Binky banter continued unabated for weeks.

"Binky loved ravioli," Ned recalled wistfully when I ordered some one evening at Pane e Vino.

"Binky loved lanterns," I heard as we perused antiques in Topanga.

"Binky loved tennis," he announced, apropos of nothing.

Wherever we went, whatever we did, the specter of Binky hovered poignantly, like Gene Tierney in *Laura*, her absence only serving to make her more present.

"Any way we could get a moratorium on all the Binky talk?"

I asked as we wandered around Pasadena one afternoon. "I'm getting a bit sick to shit of it."

"Am I talking about Binky?" Ned asked, seriously dumbfounded. "I had no idea. Yes, of course. I'm so sorry about that . . . geez . . ."

After five minutes or so of Binky-less conversation, Ned asked, "Did I ever tell you about the time Binky and I went to Joshua Tree?"

Finally, Ned left to shoot his movie. I started to spend time with Mary and Jimmie from upstairs and their adorable daughters. I learned that Jimmie was gravely ill, his condition worsening by the day. The change from when I first met him was remarkable. The big, strapping, gorgeous guy was now, only a few weeks later, a stooped-over, scary-skinny old man who hack-coughed incessantly. And he had that look in his eyes. The sunken, unmistakably dull look in his once bright, shiny eyes that I knew meant he was between two worlds. Though Jimmie spent his days writing scripts, he was also a theater director and had the most brilliant, imaginative mind. I could listen to him talk for hours. While Mary was at work and the girls were at school, I spent any lunchtime I could just sitting with him on his bed talking about plays. I would go to Erewhon, the health food store, in the mornings and get a salad for myself and Essiac tea—a blend of herbs with healing properties said to cure the most dire cancer cases—for Jimmie. Sometimes Jimmie would coach me for my auditions; sometimes he would be too weak to even talk, and we would just sit together in his darkened room, silently listening to the deluge.

"You know what I want?" Jimmie asked me one day as he looked into a bowl of veggie–bee pollen slop he had sitting in the fridge.

"No, what?"

"In-N-Out," he wheezed.

"You mean . . . a burger?"

"Yeah. I gave up eating meat 'cause I didn't want to swallow all that fear, you know?"

"Uh-huh," I said. Sure I knew.

"But now I'm like, fuck it. I really want a Double-Double."

So off we went. And just like that, we both became carnivores again.

The rain continued, and with it came the threat of mud slides. I was terrified that our decaying abode would float off the hill at any moment, but when some L.A. County official came out to inspect the premises, we were informed that our house was fine and that the only concern was that the house *above us* was liable to careen down its slope on top of us, pummeling us to smithereens.

I was grateful for the time I spent upstairs with Jimmie, Mary, and the girls, which, with Ned gone and my somber moods continuing, seemed to be happening more and more. I would sometimes watch the clock all morning, willing it to speed up so I could run out in my car to pick the girls up from their school in the canyon. Nights would be spent curled up on their sofa watching TV for hours. Jimmie's condition worsened, and various healers would show up to weigh in on what he should do and how he should focus his energy. One day, I was coming in from an audition and found him in his pajamas sitting beneath a tree, barefoot, his feet covered with mud.

"A healer was here," he said quietly. "She told me I am not grounded enough. If I want to stay in this world, I have to embrace the earth."

I sat down next to him and scooped more mud onto his feet, then took my shoes off and scooped some onto mine. We stayed there until dinner, talking about Stephen Sondheim and Jean Cocteau and how great it would be to drive around Rome in an open jeep with Anna Magnani.

Not long after, I got a call from Mary in the middle of the night: could I stay with the girls, she wanted to know. An ambulance was coming; Jimmie needed to be rushed to the hospital. It was touch and go for a few days, but finally they brought him home, and for the next week, all sorts of visitors trekked up the hill to see him. People who were dear friends and even people he hadn't talked to in years because of some terrible falling-out. Everyone, it seemed, was coming to say good-bye. Around this time, after weeks of storms, the rain miraculously stopped. Spring had arrived. The mud dried up, and jasmine once again filled the air. Jimmie, in the eleventh hour, started a new experimental drug, and his condition began to stabilize.

I spoke with my apartment swapper, who wanted to come back early; she needed to see Jimmie and be there for Mary and the girls. My father called; since my apartment swapper was leaving, would I, he wanted to know, be coming back? If not, my brother would like to take my apartment. I had only been in L.A. for six months, and while I wasn't ready to fully commit to it, I wasn't ready to leave either. I had thus far been living by my wits, pulling down the lever on the slot machine and scoring. Why not do it again?

I couldn't know then that my luck had essentially run out, and that for the next seven years I would struggle to stay sane, waylaid in a town I would end up loathing. It was all very visceral: I felt the sun; I smelled the jasmine; I looked down the hill through the palms and birds-of-paradise at the Hollywood Holiday Inn and knew exactly what people like Mary Pickford and Douglas Fairbanks and Cecil B. DeMille saw when they all trooped out from New Jersey to start Hollywood: how marvelous it was when it was clear! You could, as the song goes, see forever. I didn't know that I would only rarely have days of such clarity and boundless optimism. Most days would be opaque, murky, dusty, and pointless. Most days would be spent sitting in a seedy, sweltering Fairfax apartment with cottage cheese ceilings, sinking deeper and deeper into the depression that would engulf me. Most days in that kiln of an apartment, I would be visited by a spectral David Mamet, who would upbraid me for going down the rabbit hole, leaving me to wonder which was actually more stifling, the heat or the expectations. But right then, I could only think about how, like Jimmie, I wanted to stay in this world, embrace the earth. Hey—I had put my feet in the mud too. So, sitting on the Stevie Nicks couch, I called my father back. Yes, I told him, my brother could take the apartment. It was time to leave the hill and find a new home.

"I need to find a new place too," Ned told me when I picked him up at LAX later that week. "My lease is up, and I wanna buy a house. Maybe we could even shack up?"

"I'm not living with you," I told him. "But I'll help you look if you help me." He agreed, and we drove around the flats of Hollywood looking for "big, wide streets," as Ned referred to them, while he blathered on about "Binky this" and "Binky that."

"Go back to Binky, Ned. Seriously."

"I can't. She cheated on me, and I can't forgive that."

"I think you can and you really should. You never shut up about her; you're in love with her. Work it out somehow. Do yourself a favor, will ya?"

Ned did go back to Binky, and I signed a lease on the tiny apartment around the corner from Canter's deli that would be my home for the next three and a half years. Ned and I stayed friends for a while, but as these things generally go, we gradually fell out of touch once he and Binky married. But once, shortly before their wedding, Ned and I met at the Mandarette for old times' sake.

"It's so strange," Ned told me as we dined on our usual kung pao chicken and ginger string beans. "Now that I'm engaged, it seems like women are just falling out of trees!"

"Meaning?"

"Meaning suddenly they're everywhere, and I get hit on constantly! It's like they can smell it, that I'm taken. Women are very competitive."

"So I've heard." I sat back in my chair and looked at him. I knew I wouldn't be seeing him anymore, and I thought back to the first day I ever saw him, at the interview for his acting class when I was all of nineteen. He seemed so serious, so grown-up, back then.

"Are you stoned?" I asked him.

"A little," he smiled. "I smoked half a joint before I took a run around Lake Hollywood. Boy, the air quality looked pretty bad. Shit's gotta be bad for your lungs." He took my hand.

"Hey."

"Yeah?"

"I'd still like to take you to Joshua Tree, you know. There's nothing like sleeping in the desert . . ."

"*Plus ça change*," I thought. We got up, and Ned walked me to my car. I had to get to a party in Santa Monica, so I couldn't linger.

"See ya, Ned. Mazel tov on the engagement," I said, hugging him. "I'm real happy for you."

"Hey, thanks," he said, holding me tight. "Think about the desert. You'd really love it. Nothing like it: all those stars, the beautiful air. The whole world is there, just peaceful and right. It's really something else . . ."

"I bet it is."

I got in my car, waved, and drove toward the sun.

# 7. Friendly Fire

**I met Jane** rehearsing bit parts for *Saturday Night Live*. I was just out of NYU; she was just out of high school. We bonded in that way you do when you're marooned in a dressing room for a week, waiting to be called onto the set: both wearing head-to-toe thrift-store black, sharing smokes, and looking forward to our first "big break" airing *live* all across the country. An assistant talent coordinator told us, twenty minutes to airtime, that our sketch had been cut. I got so upset I almost threw up, but Jane was all business:

"Can we still come to the party?" she asked.

"Uh . . . no." The minion's tone was flat and crushing.

We repaired to a crappy bar for a round of kamikazes and a good cry. For several hours, we swam in a pool of sad stories from our childhoods. Jane lived on the Upper West Side with her mom, a fretful, Shelley-Winters-in-*Lolita* type who'd never recovered from being left for a younger woman by Jane's dad. She told me she missed her dad terribly and rarely got to see him since he lived in California with his new wife. She told me she hated having a big nose and a fat ass, both of which she blamed on her dad's side of the family. I told her I lived in the Village with my cat, Max; that I wanted to be a great lady of the stage like Eva Le Gallienne; and that I didn't know what the hell she was talking about: she was beautiful. Jane smiled, a preternaturally rueful smile, and said that no matter how pretty she was or could ever be, there would always be someone prettier. She said I should remember that too, as it would be "one of the suckiest things in life." We exchanged numbers. Within weeks, we were inseparable. We freelanced with the same agents. Sometimes, we went on the same auditions.

One day, Jane picked me up for a casting call. When I opened the door, her eyes bugged out, and she stuck out her tongue.

"Oh my god! You can't go like that! You can't, like, go in there with frizzy hair and no makeup and expect them to 'get it'! You really have to at least *try* to look pretty, you know? Here, let me fix you . . ."

She rewet my hair, blew it out flat as a pancake with her Mason Pearson brush, and did a quick makeup job.

"You may wanna stuff, too . . ."

"What?"

"Your boobs. It'd be better to stuff."

Why did it matter what my boobs looked like, I wanted to know. We were trying out for chorus parts in an experimental version of *Antigone*—for no pay.

"I'm not about that. I'm an *artist*. My job is to analyze the text and live truthfully under the imaginary circumstances of the play," I declaimed, giving Jane the whole Mamet spiel while she stuffed a pair of Nike tennis socks into my bra.

"Wrong," she said, adjusting me for symmetry. "Your *job* is to look fuckable. Anyway, this isn't working. The socks look lumpy. You really need those 'chicken cutlet' thingies . . ."

We didn't get the parts. They said we looked too "clean."

A few months later, in early December, Jane landed a tiny part in a play about yuppies at the Public Theater. I went to Florida for Christmas with my family, and since Jane was rehearsing her play downtown, she stayed in my apartment and fed my cat. A week later, I came home and found Jane in tears as she packed.

"I don't want to go home, Nancy," she told me through choked sobs. "I really, really don't. But I have nowhere else to go . . ."

Apparently, things had become intolerable living with her mother. They argued constantly about Jane's weight, her dad, and money. She wanted to move out, to get a place of her own, but didn't have the means.

"Crash with me," I told her. "Until you get on your feet."

Why not? The closeness we had as allies in such a crazy game—sharing our woes and boosting each other's morale—meant the world to me. Besides, I was making great money cocktail waitressing at the new "it" nightclub, my success stemming in large part from Jane's ingenious beauty tricks. I started blowing my normally wild and wavy hair stick straight and became resolutely "bangs obsessed." I started using foundation to contour the nose Jane pronounced "cute, but just a tad wide."

"We should play up your mouth," she told me, brushing gloss onto my lips. "It'll offset your nose."

When Jane suggested I wear tight, tiny T-shirts with no bra because it made my nipples look "so awesome!," I figured what the hell and did that too. Soon, I was taking home fistfuls of tips.

After Jane's play finished its run, she went back to waitressing at a burger joint. When we weren't working, we hung out all the time. We shopped together, dieted together, took aerobics classes, went to bowling parties with other actors . . . On Wednesdays, we played poker with lesbians.


When Jane's twentieth birthday came along, I threw her a party and got her a cake in the shape of a movie marquee with her name "in lights." Jane was so broke, she couldn't afford to get her cowboy boots reheeled at the cobbler near my apartment, but she still scraped enough money together to buy me an amazing pair of earrings from Putumayo as a thank-you, and also my very first thong underwear ("for tight jeans!").

In addition to the sartorial suggestions and canny beauty tips, Jane offered advice on how I could give my attitude a bit of a makeover too. One of my best friends, Michael, had recently died of AIDS at the age of twenty-two. I was totally bereft. One afternoon, I was ranting about it to Jane while she sat on the couch, languidly snipping her split ends with a pair of tiny nail scissors.

"You seem really . . . angry," Jane said, her eyes focused like lasers at the offending strands.

"Yeah, I am," I said. "Ten seconds ago, we were at Carnegie Hall watching Liza Minnelli right after she got out of rehab, and now he's dead. I can't believe I have to live out the rest of my life without him."

"But you seem like an angry person in general. I think you give off a very angry vibe, and you should, like, think about that. If you wanna be on TV, you have to be likable."

"I thought you said I had to be fuckable."

"Both. You have to be both. But you can't be fuckable if you're pissed-off seeming. Look at Justine Bateman: She seems really happy and super cute. And her career's going *great*. Something you should think about . . ."

Jane was absolutely right. I *was* angry about a lot of things: About Michael; about my lack of progress as an actor; about the fact that suddenly no one seemed to care what I thought or said, that all that mattered in the "real world" was how I looked. I was angry that Jane so blithely participated in what I viewed as the soul-crushing compulsion to be pretty and keep quiet, and that none of it seemed to faze her. I was angry that being angry wasn't OK, and I was even angry at Jane for calling me angry. But the thing was . . . her candor stopped me cold. Her tone was harsh—yes—but on some level I understood that her words were not intended as a judgment; they were meant as a caveat. She was explaining, in simple terms, what was *required of me* if I wanted to succeed. Jane's admonishments pissed me off, but in a funny way I also felt cared for—as though she was looking out for me.

Meanwhile, my home seemed to provide a safe haven for Jane, away from her mother's constant nagging and criticisms. Though she talked tough with me, Jane eased up on herself. She ate an extra helping of pasta here, a bit of chocolate cake for dessert there, and one day, her clothes stopped fitting. Stepping on the scale, she discovered to her horror that she had gained five pounds. She became terribly depressed and vowed to correct the situation immediately. But when her old dieting tricks (subsisting on diet cream soda and Merits) didn't work anymore, she eventually just gave up and started shoving Wonder Bread slathered with Hellmann's mayonnaise into her mouth in a benumbed stupor. Soon she could only wear her turquoise spandex workout pants and baggy sweaters. I listened with deteriorating patience to her complain about her nose, her weight, her ass.

"You are still a beautiful girl," I told her over and over, "I promise, you don't need to fix a thing." But it was to no avail. Jane would only stare at me, helpless and utterly despondent. Sometime in May, after having stayed with me for five months, she moved out and into her dad's house in Los Angeles. As much as I loved and cared for her, I felt relieved when she left and hoped the change would be good for both of us.

Two months later, Jane called with big news.

"I did it! I got a nose job! My dad bought it for me. I went to the same guy who did his nose, so they gave him a deal!"

She raved about the special diet she had gone on (prepackaged burgers and pancakes) and proudly reported losing fifteen pounds in only a few weeks. Her agent was sending her out on sitcom auditions and getting all kinds of amazing "feedback" from casting directors. Scripts were being messengered to her dad's house. A gig was imminent.

"It's almost as though I actually act better with my new nose—know what I mean?"

Jane and I kept in touch over the phone, and she told me all about her self-improvements: another nose job ("The first one didn't take!"), a hairline revamping ("so I don't have to have bangs!"), and a whopping thirty-five-pound weight loss. I never liked her other noses as much as I liked the original one, but she was deliriously happy, and for that I was happy too. Soon she booked a supporting role on a sitcom and got a new boyfriend. I, meanwhile, played one of the leads in an *After School Special*, did several off-off-Broadway plays, and fell in love with the Jazz Musician. Whenever Jane was in town, we would meet up in the garden of Café La Fortuna for skim milk café au laits.

When I decided to move to L.A., Jane had just landed her first leading role on a hot new sitcom. We arranged to have lunch at Revival Café on Beverly. Jane ordered for both of us: scrambled egg whites cooked in "low oil" and bagels scooped of all their bread, so all that remained was a bagel shell. I had recently guest-starred on *Seinfeld*, and Jane was incredulous.

"You've only been here, like, what? Two months? How awesome!"

Though buoyed by the guest spot, I was still broke and feeling anxious about the move to L.A. And logistically, I only had another month to house-sit for a friend. I needed a place to stay, even briefly. I told Jane my dilemma.

"I don't know what to do," I said. "I don't have anywhere to go . . ."

She furrowed her brow, fired up a Merit, and thought for a minute. Finally, it dawned on her.

"Of course! You should stay at the Oakwood! Have you heard of it? It's temporary housing just off Laurel Canyon!"

We finished up our egg whites and bagel shells, and I walked her to her Range Rover.

"You seem really great, Jane. Really, just so great," I said, hugging her. She smiled warmly and scrunched up her new nose at me.

"It's 'cause I'm not desperate anymore," she said and looked at me meaningfully, as though I were an errant child who needed gentle reminders of boundaries.

"Desperation freaks people out, especially out here. This was so fun. Let's do it again real soon . . ."

Jane's show became the breakout hit of the season, a sensation. She had done it: Jane was a star. I called her several times, leaving messages of congratulations. She didn't return my calls. One day, I got her on the phone.

"I'm SO SORRY!" she cried, hearing my voice. "EVERYONE is pissed at me! All my friends. I never call anyone back. I'm just so busy! But I'd love to see you—can we do next Thursday?"

But on Thursday, something came up, and Jane said we'd have to reschedule.

A month later, I coincidentally had a meeting with the casting director for Jane's show.

"There's a great part we're casting for the last episode of the season. You'd be perfect. Can you stick around here, take a look at the script, and meet the producers at two?"

I went in for the audition, and a few hours later I received the Call: I was hired. I was told to report to the studio the next day at nine A.M. to begin a week of work. I was being paid more money than I'd ever made in my career. I called Jane and got her machine. I left a message saying I'd booked the job, I was thrilled, and I'd see her the next day. A few hours later, the casting director called me.

"Nancy . . . I'm so sorry, there's been a . . . a change. They've cut your part. You'll still be paid, for the full week. Everyone feels so bad. I'm sorry."

The casting director went on to say that the producers had assured her they would cast me in another episode the following season. I tried to console myself with the promise of a future role.

Later that week, I went out to dinner with my old friend Gabe, who had become a successful TV producer. After I told him the story, he shook his head.

"That doesn't make sense. Why'd they pay you so much when they didn't use you, especially when they said they'd bring you on next year?"

Gabe knew the producers of Jane's show; he said he'd see what he could find out. A few days later, he took me to lunch.

"She had you fired," he said.

"Who?" I asked.

"Jane. She told them that she wouldn't work with you."

"What? Why? And, they'll just do what she says? Aren't they her bosses?"

"She's one of the stars of the show. Believe me, she gets whatever she wants. She wants someone fired, boom, they're gone. But I don't get it. Why? I thought you guys were close.

Didn't she live with you? Did you have some kind of falling-out?"

"You mean there was no 'script change'?" I asked, struggling to make sense of it.

Gabe shook his head. "Nah. They just . . . they had to re-cast."

"So . . . then . . . there'll be no next season either?"

Gabe shook his head.

I started to cry. I was devastated.

"It sucks, I know," he said, taking my hand. "I'm real sorry. This business is, you know . . . whaddaya gonna do . . ."

I called Jane and left messages wanting to know what happened; she didn't return my calls.

I never spoke to her again.

Jane would go on to superstardom, marry a hunky guy, win several awards. I, on the other hand, would sputter along, stopping and starting, sometimes playing along with the game, sometimes recoiling in ambivalence. But whatever I did in the years that followed our friendship, I was never without a Mason Pearson brush, and I always had *great hair*.


A few years ago, when Jane went through a nasty and very tabloidy divorce—her husband having left her for a younger woman—people would call me up all the time, asking if I was experiencing a spectacular episode of schadenfreude. The answer was no. Maybe it's natural for people to assume that her misfortunes would somehow be satisfying to me, but here is the truth. Whenever she comes up, I can only think of Jane as I knew her: a sweet, hopelessly insecure girl who yearned for her dad, wanted above all to make herself pretty, pretty, pretty, and was willing to sacrifice pieces of herself to do so. She was someone I

liked knowing, someone with whom I had a great deal in common and, at the same time, nothing at all. Nevertheless, we
shared a period of time, had some fun, and helped each other just
a little in the best way we knew how. She was someone I considered a true friend, and no matter how hard I try, I can never, ever
forget that. So, when I think of Jane, I just feel sad.

I once read an interview with Jane where she said that if her career hadn't worked out, she'd have been happy just serving people burgers at the joint she worked at all those years ago when
she was shacking up with me. She said she got joy out of just
giving people fries and milk shakes and getting tips. It felt honest to her, and somehow, she felt as though she forged friend-
ships with the customers that were very deep. I know what she
meant. There are those connections you have with people that
on the surface seem fleeting, ephemeral, inexplicable, but that
you nonetheless feel certain are important and terribly profound
and very real, until one day when you look back on it and you
think to yourself . . . maybe not. Anyway, I would imagine that
deep down Jane knows—as I do—that even if it were that simple, sometimes being a friend is just not enough. And that is one
of the suckiest things in life.

## 8. I Am What I Am

**No one is** immune to the lure of stardom. Even when you think you know yourself—and that you're happy with your little life in the shadows—if met with the unexpected prospect of fame and overnight success, you see things very differently. That's what happened to my friend T.J. T.J. was just a regular schmo working two jobs: one as the personal assistant to "Mama" Michelle Phillips of the Mamas and the Papas, and the other as the maître d'/wine captain at Morton's steakhouse on La Cienega. The Mama Michelle gig was surprisingly great; Michelle was cool and generous, a rare celebrity who, though well aware of her fabulousness, never expected her employees or anyone else to revel in her impudence. Of course, Michelle was stoned all day long, which may have accounted for her loveliness in part, as well as the fact that she cooked some seriously badass Mexican food.

Once, when I was over at her place visiting T.J., he got a call from a ladies' magazine that wanted Michelle to describe her "beauty regimen."

"Are you serious?" she asked T.J., fixing her luminous blue eyes on him. She was still in her white robe with her hair wrapped in a towel from her morning shower, sitting at the kitchen table, drinking coffee and rolling a joint.

"That's what they wanna know," T.J. continued, pen poised on his notepad.

"Tell them that when I wake up in the morning, the first thing I do is weigh myself. If I'm an ounce over 122, I pop a Dexie. Then I get stoned and have a vodka. Later I get stoned some more. Then I make some fish tacos at around five, have some more vodka until I pass out. That's about it. Oh, and I sleep with a plastic surgeon . . ."

Because the Mama Michelle gig wasn't regular, T.J. also had to take the Morton's job. It paid well enough, but unlike at Michelle's, where anything went, at Morton's there were all sorts of stuffy rules and protocols. Everyone had to have their apron on just so, the right shoes, the flawless ability to appear in a flash and then vanish. Servers were required to memorize the entire menu and recite it with dramatic reverence and swooping crescendos, while wielding bloody porterhouse props. I called these mini-productions "Cirque du Soleil: The Monologue." The obsequious pyrotechnics expected of the Morton's staffers made sense, since the restaurant catered to the peevish, tight-faced denizens of Beverly Hills and scores of bratty, overindulged celebrities. The waiters didn't mind it; they all wanted to be actors, and this was their time to perform. But not T.J. T.J. didn't want to be an actor at all. His dream was to be a theater producer. All through our years at NYU, he produced student shows. His posters bore a trademark that became legendary: T.J.'s name in bold, followed by an even bolder "PRESENTS." I'm not sure how many people actually saw his shows, but everyone knew those posters. People even started referring to him as Presents, his nickname to this day. But after a postgraduation attempt to bring a revival of *Hair* back to the New York stage went seriously awry, T.J. ran away to Key West. For seven years, he worked in a hotel bar and lived in a seaside efficiency flat, drowning his producing dreams in the salty surf and his sorrows in Tanqueray. Eventually, our friend Matthew coaxed T.J. out to Los Angeles, where he got a job working as the assistant to a talent agent and rented a sweetly shabby six-hundred-dollar apartment in back of the Scientology Center. Though soot and exhaust piled up on his windowsills daily—the price of living beneath the Hollywood freeway—it was home.

Soon after T.J. arrived, the talent agent came under investigation for allegedly cashing in his client's paychecks, the agency shut its doors, and T.J. was, once again, out of a job. But Mama Michelle came to the rescue, the Morton's job came through, and finally, it looked as though T.J. was on the up-and-up. All he wanted was to get on his feet, make his car payments and rent, buy fresh flowers occasionally, have friends to dinner—the trappings of a nice, quiet life.

One night at Morton's, several months after he was hired, T.J. was waiting on a party of six celebrating a birthday.

"The reservation was under the name Nikki Haskell," T.J. said when he called me later. "She was in position one, and the gentleman whose birthday it was, was in position two," he explained, using restaurant parlance to describe who was sitting where at the table. "So, they're done, and out comes the dessert with a candle, and of course, we're all singing 'Happy Birthday.' When we finish, Miss Haskell starts shrieking, *'OH COME ON! THAT'S THE BEST YOU CAN DO? IT'S ALLAN CARR, FOR CHRISSAKES!'*"

"No way," I said, laughing. "Allan Carr?"

This was a huge deal. T.J. really admired Allan Carr: he was a tremendously successful producer and talent manager. Short, stout, stomach-stapled, with a face resembling that of a benign sea monster, Allan Carr epitomized the excess of Celebrity, with his fabulously flamboyant lifestyle replete with billowy caftans, floor-length furs, and lavish theme parties thrown in his Egyptian-style home disco.

Surrounded by famous friends and young lovers, Allan Carr lived a charmed life; the world was his deep-fried oyster. It *was*, anyway, until the end of the eighties, when Carr was asked to produce the Oscars, the one where Rob Lowe sang "Proud Mary" to Snow White. While I actually thought this Debbie Allen–choreographed smorgasbord bordered on genius, the rest of the world disagreed: it was universally derided as an unmitigated disaster and the tackiest Academy Awards in history, quite a feat, given the level of taste for which the Oscars are usually known. After that, Carr's career was over; he never worked in Hollywood again.

But T.J. didn't care. To him, Allan Carr would always be the guy who cast Olivia Newton-John opposite John Travolta in *Grease*; the guy who knew Broadway audiences would embrace the gay couple in *La Cage aux Folles*; the guy who discovered Steve Guttenberg. So what if Carr was, by this point, just another washed-up queen relegated to overpaying for strip steak and baked potato? To T.J., it didn't matter a whit. He knew Hollywood was a cruel place, but he also knew it was a place where you could have a second act. A place where you could reinvent yourself. T.J. felt a kinship with Carr and wanted him to know it was OK: he might be down-and-out, but surely, some day soon, he'd have a comeback. In T.J.'s eyes, Allan Carr was still a hero. So, with nary a moment's hesitation, T.J. began to sing the eleven o'clock number from *La Cage*:

*I am what I am, I am my own special creation*
*So come take a look, give me the hook or the ovation*
*It's my world that I want to have a little pride in*
*My world and it's not a place I have to hide in*

*Life's not worth a damn 'til you can say, hey world*
*I am what I am . . .*

The entire restaurant stopped to watch what was, according to one of the waiters who witnessed it, a purely spontaneous yet riveting performance. When it was over, as T.J. held the last note and exited with a graceful flourish through the swinging doors of the Morton's kitchen, the restaurant patrons erupted in frenzied applause.

"It was incredible," T.J. said. "They were hooting and hollering, whistling and carrying on."

"Wow," I said.

"Allan Carr was crying . . ."

"Wow," I repeated.

"So then, Nikki Haskell pulls me aside and says, 'What you did over there was just amazing. Allan was so moved.' So I said, 'Well, goodness, thank you, Miss Haskell. You know, I'm quite a fan of Allan's—and of yours as well.' "

"Is he kidding?" I thought. "*Nikki Haskell?* That diet pill lady with the eighties fright hair whose mug looms over Sunset Boulevard?"

"So then," T.J. said, "she asked me to come to Allan's official birthday luncheon, next week at Le Dome. She wants me to re-create the performance I did tonight, only this time in drag."

"Oh. My. God. What did you say?"

"Nothing. I was floored. Then she says, 'I've got an accompanist, and I can pay you one hundred dollars, but really, this shouldn't be about money. This is a *big deal* for you: Allan Carr can make you a *star*. It's as simple as that. There are going to be MAJOR, MAJOR celebrities there, and, well, this is a *life-changing* thing for you, really.' "

"Wow."

"Can you believe it, Nancy?" he asked, sounding on the verge of either laughing or crying. "Tonight, I was *discovered*."

That Nikki Haskell's blandishments really meant anything to him beyond chatter I found completely shocking, but T.J. seemed to be really taking this thing to heart. More curiously, T.J. wasn't even an actor. I'd had no idea that he harbored dreams of performing, let alone stardom. It wasn't that I didn't think T.J. was lovable; he had a certain spark and boyish charm that I always found irresistible. Who was to say others wouldn't see the same thing? Maybe they already had. Still, I was amazed by how quickly he had gotten the star bug.

"Anyway," T.J. continued, "I said yes, of course. I mean— what else could I say? Which is, by the way, why I'm calling you at this ungodly hour: are you gonna get over here and help me or what? I'm completely freaking out . . ."

After throwing on some clothes, I headed to T.J.'s apartment in my marginally running Rabbit convertible. I wanted to feel nothing but delight for T.J.; maybe fate had smiled on him— finally—bringing his run of bad luck to an end, the Carr episode heralding the dawn of an exhilarating epoch. But as I imagined the pages turning to a new chapter for T.J., an unfamiliar feeling arose, a feeling I had previously believed myself to be immune to: *envy*. I had always been glad for people—especially friends—when they got the things they wanted. "No need to covet; there is enough for everyone" was always my mantra. Pollyannaish, maybe—perhaps even delusional—but it was how I felt.

But so much had changed. I was in that terrible place an actor gets to in L.A. where you've been out there for a year or so and, after an initial slew of work, everything seems to have dried up. You're not getting cast, you're not being seen for this project or that, and you're constantly in fear of your agent dropping you. Maybe you've put on a bit of weight, which makes you even nuttier. You are desperate and bored, languishing away with resentment and paranoia that the whole Hollywood thing is a lie. Because you bought the swampland. Everybody else's win is your loss. You're rotting away drinking Vanilla Blendeds by day and dirty martinis by night, talking bitterly about what you "deserve."

Driving up Highland, toward the Hollywood hinterlands, I found myself all of a sudden doing the second most common activity I did on a daily basis besides driving: crying. And more and more, I was doing these acts concurrently. Two years had passed since I'd been fired from my friend Jane's hit TV show, and unbelievably, I still had not fully recovered from the pain and humiliation. I still had trouble believing the story that she had instigated my release, but regardless, I had lost my mojo entirely, stopped getting work, and fallen into a deep, unshakable depression. To pay my rent, I would participate in bogus focus groups with other out-of-work actors, pretending to advertising executives and their clients hidden behind two-way mirrors that I adored a gin I had never even tried, and when I wasn't doing that, I was blow-drying other actresses' hair in my kitchen for twenty dollars a pop, using the techniques Jane had taught me all those years before. Occasionally, I booked commercial voice-overs where I would sit in a booth extolling the virtues of cereal or kitty litter or twenty-four-hour Mormon banks, then afterward drive around on broad, dusk-illuminated Los Angeles streets named for flowers and saints and swamps, crying and driving, driving and crying, thinking, rationalizing, searching. Nowhere was the clarity of those early L.A. days of promise, the ones when I could see all the way down the hills. Now I lived in the flats: there was nothing to see. And even if there were, clarity, I would come to find out, was anomalous: most days a dull film etched a stark silhouette against the sky, hovering over the whole city, nowhere to go. *Smog,* everyone said it was *smog.* Pretty soon, however, I came to think that what got trapped in that vast Los Angeles basin wasn't smog at all, but the psychic haze of collective despair. And now, some of it was mine.

Pulling onto T.J.'s street, I thought about how, more than anyone else in my life during those dog days, T.J. was there for me, making me laugh with his diversionary antics, his adorable grin, and his general craziness, all of which made me feel not so all alone. I loved T.J.; I wanted him to shine, to succeed, to have everything he ever dreamed of. These sickening green-eyed pangs had nothing to do with him, I told myself, and everything to do with how terrible I felt about myself.

When I got to T.J.'s apartment, I found him sitting on his corduroy sofa—still in his Morton's tux—drinking a beer. He was listening to the sound track to *La Cage* on a boom box. I sat next to him and took a sip of the beer. We sat listening for a few minutes, not speaking, until finally T.J. got up and clicked off the boom box.

"I need you to direct me," he said. "I need you to help me re-create what I did tonight."

"Sure," I told him. T.J. seemed shaken, somehow. As though his new life as a superstar was already a burden for him.

"I'll split the hundred bucks with you, OK?"

"Sure."

T.J. was wandering around in circles now.

"I need a beer," he said absently.

"Whatsa matter with that one?" I asked, gesturing toward the half-full bottle in his hand.

"Huh?" He looked down at his beer. "I guess I'm just kind of scared," he shrugged. "What if I can't do it again? What if it was just a fluke?"

"Look," I told him, channeling Mama Rose in *Gypsy*, "it's in you. You did it tonight. Nothing to be afraid of. We'll work it and work it some more until you're good and comfortable. You'll blow them away just like tonight. 'Kay?"

The truth was that a part of me *did* think it was a fluke, but another part of me thought it was entirely possible that something very real had clicked for T.J. and that perhaps by some strange alchemy, his lack of pretense—not to mention lack of experience—had produced a small miracle. Yes, he had sung in his high school glee club and at piano bars when he was tanked enough, but this was different. Something in the nether crevices of T.J.'s soul connected to the raw emotions of what the iconic anthem he had sung meant: Be Proud, Be Unabashed, Be Yourself. It all started to click: I grew excited thinking of the possibilities of directing T.J., not just this once, but as the start of something new, maybe even a whole act that I could inject myself into. "Maybe," I thought, "T.J.'s budding success could do something for *my* acting career." As soon as the thought entered my mind, I scolded myself. What was happening to me? I was disturbed at how mercenary I felt, how opportunistic and grabby, especially when I wasn't even sold that this Carr thing had legs. It was like in that old Bugs Bunny episode about being stranded on a deserted island and seeing your equally starved, emaciated friend as a mirage of a plump, juicy roast. I hated myself for viewing T.J.—the Wind Beneath My Wings—as dinner. "No," I thought, "be a friend. Be here for T.J." Besides, extrapolating further, I knew that later, after he was secure in his fame and ensconced in his new flashy life, I would still be one of his best friends and, perhaps, even his artistic partner-in-crime. I pictured us in the afterglow of his triumphant performance— the "Le Dome performance," we'd come to call it—basking in the reflected glory of all those big stars Nikki Haskell had promised. I saw us kibitzing with Jack and Warren, trading fours with Marlon and Meryl, giggling with Goldie. I was even excited to meet Steve Guttenberg; I loved him in *Diner*! I had always firmly believed that zeitgeist was contagious—if something spectacular happens to someone to whom you are close, you're next. As I watched T.J. toss back beer after beer, I wondered if Nikki Haskell had been right after all and this *was* a life-changing moment. Perhaps for all of us.

For the next week, T.J. and I set about turning him into a seasoned drag queen. We went to a wholesale place in downtown L.A. to buy a blond wig, bought seamed panty hose, and borrowed a dress, high heels, and a bra with fake tits from Matthew, who for some reason was in possession of these items. Michelle lent us a boa and some earrings, and we made an appointment with my eyebrow lady for some shaping and unibrow expunging. Then we rehearsed. Or we tried to. T.J. kept getting distracted and stopping mid-run-through to take phone calls from friends:

". . . And then I just said, 'You know, NIKKI, it's hard for me to talk about my PROCESS, but I really become that other person. Everything just strips away. It's me—yes—but it's also not me, if that makes sense . . .'"

T.J. embellished the Allan Carr Story with each retelling. In some versions, even the recessed lighting at Morton's cooperated, bathing him in a glorious pool of blue-gold. In other versions, he sounded like he was describing Judy Garland in her famous Palace performances, when she'd sit on the edge of the stage in her clown getup, with just a tiny pin light on her sad little rouged face, singing "Over the Rainbow."

Listening to him repeat the story, it occurred to me that T.J. was buying into his own hype. Maybe, I reasoned, this was how people actually became stars: they might be just normal at first, but then, something snapped, be it an opportunity they were ready to seize or the perfect confluence of events, chance, talent, and luck. But one thing was for sure: if they didn't start believing it all themselves, they were sunk. I thought back to that scene in *Truth or Dare* where Madonna is sitting on her bed with her two backup singers, and she admits she has moments of doubt, but knows she can never give in to it or the jig is up; if she dares to let those negative thoughts in—even a little—how will she ever be able to get up onstage, let alone writhe around in that conical Gaultier bra during the "Like a Virgin" "masturbation scene"?

I remembered this guy from NYU who was a pathological liar; he'd miss scene study class, and when questioned as to where he'd been, he'd say something ludicrous like, "I was shooting a movie with Bobby De Niro." "He's really crazy," we'd all think. "How sad!" But then, ten years later, he really *was* making movies with De Niro, which got me to thinking that perhaps pathological liars weren't really liars at all. They might just be seers, able to divine what was in store. Or, maybe they were such good liars that they themselves believed what came out of their mouths and just made it eventually come true. Either way, it became clear that what was most essential was to *believe*. And that belief had to be so profound, so unwavering, that nothing could stop the inevitable. T.J.'s humility, his self-deprecating aw-shucks demeanor, was nowhere to be found, and perhaps, I thought, this was a good thing. Still, I knew he desperately needed to rehearse. But every time I chimed in about it, he got snippy with me; I was starting to feel like his personal assistant.

"He's behaving like a douche," Matthew said when I called him to complain. "He needs to just get over himself."

Part of me agreed with Matthew, but as T.J.'s Allan Carr

Story began to circulate, other friends started seeing T.J. anew. Over the years, as people lamented his various fiascoes, the oft-repeated refrain was "Aw, jeez, poor T.J. . . ." Now, in the span of a few days, T.J. had morphed into a full-throttle diva, and these same people who had pitied him were brimming with appreciation—awe, even.

"Does anyone have a buckwheat pillow? I need it for my neck," T.J. asked one night after a dinner in his honor. All evening, he'd been throwing his weight around, alternately demanding things and, just as capriciously, staring off into space, a genius, lost in thought.

"I don't know how you put up with him," Matthew said, driving me home that night.

"It's just nerves," I said. And while I certainly wasn't thrilled with how T.J. was acting, I knew he didn't mean it. He was just reeling from all the pressure.

We stayed up all night before the Allan Carr event, fine-tuning T.J.'s costume and choreography. I worked out this cute bit where, toward the end of the number, having approached Allan Carr's table, and singing directly to him, T.J. would glide around behind Allan's chair and gently drape the boa around his neck. Then he was to caress Allan's cheeks, turn, face the room, and chuckle a mirthless little chuckle while taking off his clip-on cloisonné earrings. Examining the earrings, as though they were not merely objects of artifice but dear friends, he would brighten, revealing his undying survivor spirit, rip off the wig, and explode the final "I AM WHAT I AM!" in an electrifying, note-holding vibrato. OK, maybe it was a little contrived. But I figured that with T.J.'s savantlike ability to connect lyrics to soul, it could work.

The next day, we drove in silence down Sunset Boulevard to Le Dome, too wound up with anticipation and fatigue to chat.

We walked through the restaurant—a garish joint with the overly art-directed look of a Nixon-era whorehouse—and found a dour fellow who resembled Vincent Price. It was the maître d'.

"Miss Haskell is waiting for you in the dining room," he slurred lugubriously.

Although she appeared more diminutive than she did on her billboards, with all that big, inky hair, Nikki Haskell was somehow much scarier in person. We found her standing by the piano rehearsing a ditty with the accompanist and a few other excessively moussed ladies. She waved when she saw T.J. and motioned for us to sit. Someone had written naughty alternate lyrics to one of the songs from *Grease* that referred to Allan Carr's penchant for food and sex. Nikki and co. giggled uproariously as they ran through it. Everyone was very tan. When they were finished, we worked out a good key for T.J.'s number, but after a few bars, feeling he needed to conserve his energy, he wanted to stop. We went off in search of a dressing room. We found a busboy vacuuming and asked him to help, but since he didn't speak English he could only look at us blankly. I told T.J. to stay put and went back to consult with Nikki.

"*Dressing room?*" she spat, looking me up and down. "What the hell do you think this is, the Copacabana?" She waved her red talons dismissively. "Listen, you'll be lucky to find a *closet* he can use." She continued, gesticulating like Edward Scissorhands in a power suit, "I don't want Allan seeing him before the performance. The whole *goddamn* thing is supposed to be a surprise!"

Whereupon, "Vincent Price" slunk over and told me we could use the bathroom that was just off the kitchen.

"Perfect," Nikki declared. "He can make his entrance from there, too." Then she turned away from me to greet Tina Sinatra, who had just arrived.

The bathroom was a two-by-two-foot room with a teensy, chipped enamel sink, a toilet, and a large plunger. For the next hour and a half, T.J. sat on the toilet with me crouched in front of him, painstakingly applying makeup and glitter. We somehow got him into his costume—which required opening the door to get more arm and head room, to the bemusement of the kitchen staff—and I went out to the bar to get him tea with lemon, honey, and bourbon.

"UGH! This tea is AWFUL!" T.J. moaned when I got back.

"Whatsa matter with it?"

"I need more honey!" he snapped, tossing the spoon in the sink. "And lemon. And water! Where is my water? How am I supposed to—"

Just then, in the midst of T.J.'s tantrum, the door to our toilet cubicle was suddenly flung open, and we were face-to-face with Joan Collins. She was in a crisp white suit, cinched at the waist, and a wide, white-brimmed hat. Her makeup was flawless. She looked like she was attending Ascot.

"*Wot's this?*" she chirped, eyes bugging out at T.J. in his dress. "Wot are you lot up to? I—I—" she sputtered. "But I thought this was the *loo.*"

T.J., miraculously regaining his composure, extended his hand as though he were the Duchess of York.

"Miss Collins," he deadpanned. "How good of you to come."

T.J. and Joan clasped hands like long-lost pals. We explained that T.J. was moments away from performing the tune from *La Cage* for Allan as a birthday gift.

"It's a surprise," I told her.

"My *gawd*," Joan's thyroidy green eyes bugged out some more. "Well, tick-a-lock, I won't say a *wuhd*!"

"Bless you, Miss Collins," T.J. curtsied, spilling his tea on one of his sling-backs.

"But," Joan stage-whispered, conspiratorially looking toward the dining room, "you *shan't* start without me, and I simply *must* dash to the *loo*!"

Joan Collins and her bladder would supply comic fodder for months afterward. At least once a day, calling T.J.'s answering machine, I would chatter away as Joan, simultaneously flushing my toilet over and over:

"Hullo, T.J. dahling! [*WHOOSH, WHOOSH.*] I'm in the loo, dahling! [*WHOOSH.*] Anyway, luv, was just coming round to your flat when I realized I simply couldn't hold it in and had to stop at the petrol station to have a tinkle. [*WHOOSH, WHOOSH.*] Anyhoo, be over shortly! Ta-ta! [*WHOOSH.*]"

We promised Joan we would hold the "curtain" until she emptied her bladder.

"Ooooh! Bless you, my *dahlings*, bless youuuuuuu!" And then, blowing a kiss over her shoulder, she scampered off.

I looked at T.J.

"'Miss Collins,'" I said, imitating him, "'how good of you to come.' Excuse me while I vomit."

"I don't have the slightest idea what you're talking about," T.J. said to his reflection in the mirror, dabbing the sweat off his upper lip with a hankie.

"Save it, sister," I said, lighting a cigarette.

"Ugh! Can you PLEASE not smoke in my dressing room?"

There was a knock on the door; we opened it. It was Joan.

"Em . . . where exactly *is* the loo?"

"Downstairs," I told her.

After she left, I went to check on where we were time-wise in the festivities and how long before T.J. was on. Peeking out from the kitchen, I saw them all: Allan Carr, Jerry Herman, Joan Collins, Suzanne Pleshette, Angie Dickinson, Nancy and Tina

Sinatra—a Who's Who of sixties kitsch, all looking more or less like themselves, just puffier. Except for Angie Dickinson. She looked exactly the same as she did as Pepper on *Police Woman*. Same hair, same tits, same world-weary-do-I-have-to-play-a-hooker-again-this-week smirk. She looked great!

"Who's out there?" T.J. asked me when I returned with the five-minute warning.

"No one," I said, not wanting to rattle him with the laundry list. "I mean, there's people, and some you know, but no biggie . . ."

"Any major celebs?" he asked, winking.

"Nope, not yet," I said. "But you know how those people always slip in at the last minute."

"True, true."

T.J. sighed deeply, then sat down on the toilet.

"What is it?" I asked.

He shook his head.

"Nothing," he said, looking at me silently for a few seconds. Then, looking away and shrugging, he grabbed my Shiseido compact. "Gosh," he said, gazing at himself in the tiny mirror. "Don't know why I didn't notice this before . . ."

"What?"

"I look exactly like my mother."

Aside from the glitter, slick red lips, and boa, T.J. looked a bit more conservative as a lady than I had originally conceptualized. He sort of looked like a wanton home ec teacher.

"I look pretty," he said finally.

"You sure do, T.J.," I said, picking a stray eyelash off his cheek. "Here," I added, holding it on my finger. "Make a wish and blow."

There was a knock; it was the maître d'.

"You're on next."

We stood behind the kitchen door listening to the accompanist vamping the intro to T.J.'s number.

*Ba-dum badum badum bum. Ba-dum badum badum bum. Ba-dum badum badum bum.*

"Remember," I told him, draping the boa around his neck, "make sure you look him in the eye, *then* drape the boa around his neck, you know? Sell it!"

T.J. nodded. Nikki announced his name, and he marched through the kitchen doors. I followed and crouched down, so that I had a stage-left view of T.J. and a direct view of the audience. There were ten or so round tables; Allan Carr was at the center table next to a few youngish-looking guys. Nikki was seated opposite him.

T.J. got into place and looked up at the "imaginary best friend" we had talked about in rehearsals. I had told him that he needed to make sure he found his light, that it should feel like the sun, warming the bridge of his nose.

*Ba-dum badum badum bum. Ba-dum badum badum bum.*

The vamping continued as T.J. bobbed his head up and down, trying to feel the light, but since there really wasn't any light—or there was; it just wasn't a key light or a special—T.J. looked like a hound trying to catch a scent.

*Ba-dum badum badum bum. Ba-dum badum badum bum.*

The room quieted to a hush. A photographer named Maureen, who we found out later was once Cary Grant's girlfriend, snapped a few photos, her flash bursting like fireflies. And then, T.J. began to sing. He was so tentative—so quiet and small—it was as though it were some kind of mistake, something we shouldn't have been privy to. Like one of those Strasberg "private moment" exercises where you watch someone pretending to do the dishes, and then the teacher—usually some hoary old commie eating a bruised banana—asks the actor being observed to "sing a little something" while doing their "activity." For all of his horn blowing, T.J. was blowing it; he was dazed with terror. And not being a real performer, he had no automatic pilot to resort to. "Make it stop," I thought. "Make it rewind."

As T.J. whispered the lyrics in a stupor, with only a hint of a voice, I anxiously watched the audience. Suzanne Pleshette was into it for a few seconds, but then just gave up and buttered a roll; Nancy Sinatra fished for something in her handbag; Angie Dickinson looked, well, just like she did on *Police Woman*; and Allan Carr stared straight ahead, expressionless. Then T.J. skulked toward Allan for the pièce de résistance moment with the boa. By now, Allan was talking to the youngish guy on his right. T.J. minced around the table.

*I am what I am and what I am needs no excuses*
*I deal my own deck sometimes the ace, sometimes the deuces*

Grabbing Allan's face, into which had just been shoved an enormous forkful of poached salmon in champagne mango emulsion, he croaked,

*There's one life and there's no return and no deposit*
*One life so it's time to open up your closet*

Allan looked a little scared but kept chewing. After T.J. let go of his face, he went back to his conversation, never looking at T.J. again. Then T.J., running out of time, threw the boa at Allan's head before limping back to the piano. A busboy tried to hand him a drink but then, realizing it was for the accompanist, scurried out of the way as T.J. valiantly squawked out the last lyric:

*Life's not worth a damn 'til you can say, hey world*
*I am what I am*

Because T.J. didn't have enough breath to sustain the last note for the planned mind-blowing finale, the accompanist covered by modulating the final notes in that two-fisted Broadway style, concluding with an extravagant *BUM-BUM BUM*. There was some polite applause. A cake was wheeled in; the accompanist started playing "Happy Birthday." Everyone sang. It was over.

I watched people milling around, eating cake, swallowing champagne. Standing on the periphery, I started to wake from the dream: There would be no kibitzing or cavorting, no partners-in-crime Hollywood success story, no follow-up act. T.J. was never going to be a star. There would be no coattails to feel guilty about attaching myself to. It was absurd, the whole thing, really, and in a sense, not much different than any other day in L.A. I watched one of Allan's young male companions helping him up out of his seat. It looked like it took great effort to haul him up, and not just because he was chubby; the heaviness he carried on his frame was clearly the weight of defeat.

Deciding to salvage a little something, I suppose, I had Maureen take a picture of me and Nancy Sinatra with our arms around each other: "Two Nancys with a Laughing Face!" we joked. Then I went to find T.J. He was at the bar, drinking a glass of wine and talking to the bartender.

"Hey!" he said cheerfully as I approached. "Mark here was just telling me that he used to know Sammy Davis Jr.!"

"Oh yeah?" I said, taking a sip of T.J.'s wine. "Cool."

"And of course, I was telling him what big fans we are and how we sing all his tunes!"

T.J. started singing "I Gotta Be Me." He was big and bold and he meant every word. I didn't have the heart to tell him it was too late.

Nikki Haskell swept into the bar on her way out to give T.J. his hundred bucks.

"Thanks," she said flatly, looking through him, then gliding off.

A few hours later, we were still at the bar. Maureen the photographer was furious.

"How dare that *cunt* Nikki Haskell treat me like the bloody *hired help*!" she ranted. "I am not *just a photographer*! I *know* these people; we used to *socialize*!" On and on she bitched and moaned.

The Le Dome staffers were methodically setting up for the dinner shift. T.J. sat on his stool, a star manqué, staring at his reflection in the mirror behind the bar, amidst the shiny liquor bottles, twirling the wine glass stem between his fingers. He was back in his khakis and a Brooks Brothers baby blue oxford, but his slack face was streaked with mascara, thick pancake makeup, and remnants of glitter. He had wiped off his red lipstick, but his lips were still bright red, as though they, too, couldn't quite let go.

Maureen left, and the bartender put on a Jo Stafford CD. The first track was "The Party's Over."

We sat silently for a few minutes, listening to Jo's lush voice, finishing our wine.

"You know," T.J. said, nudging me, "Angie Dickinson said I was amazing. She came up to me on her way out and said, 'You were so great. It's *really, really, REALLY* nice to meet you.'"

I nodded. "She seems cool."

"Oh," T.J. said, nodding his head vigorously, "*very.*"

Jo finished her song and began another.

"Here," T.J. said, sighing heavily and handing me fifty bucks.

"Thanks," I said, getting off the stool. "You wanna have a bite? I'm starved."

"I'd love to," he said. "But I'm . . . I'm . . ." He shook his head.

"What?"

"I don't have any money," he said finally. "I spent it all at the bar."

I smiled at him. As ludicrous as it seems, I was having trouble letting go of T.J.'s star status myself. Only hours before, he'd had the whole world in the palm of his hand. Or had he? Allan Carr was in no more position than I was to change someone's life with the snap of his fingers. He was a defrocked starmaker. Either way, I thought, as we packed up our junk and T.J. took one last look around the tacky dining room, nothing is for keeps. Except maybe an ashtray.

"Here," T.J. said, handing me one he'd snatched off a table. "Put this in your bag."

"Come on," I said, wrapping the ashtray in Mama Michelle's boa, then putting my arm through his. "Let's go to Denny's. We'll order some Moons over My Hammy, my treat."

We left the way we came: through the kitchen.

"You know, at first I thought maybe I kind of blew it," T.J. said as we slid into his car. "But Angie was so enthusiastic, you know?"

I nodded.

"Goes to show, you never can tell." T.J. shifted the car into gear. "You just never can . . ."

We drove slowly out of the back parking lot, wending our way toward Hollywood as the sun, a smudgy blood orange orb, slipped away behind the giant palms on Sunset Boulevard.

## 9. Fen-phen Made Me Fat!
## (Easter in Vegas, 1996)

**I honestly don't** remember why I decided to go to Vegas with T.J. I guess I was restless, needed to get out of L.A. for a minute, and since I'd had fun there once before, I figured, why not? There's something oddly cleansing about the spectacularly tawdry splendor of Vegas, attracting the fat, the high-rolling, the middling, the fanny-packed, the lost, all collectively shaking out their weary souls like dirty welcome mats. Bets are on, so all bets are off.

"I got us a room opposite Caesar's," T.J. said. "There's air-conditioning, free breakfast, and porn."

We left on Good Friday, two days before Easter, at around noon, stopping first at the Rexall pharmacy on Beverly so I could pick up my third prescription for fen-phen. It was the middle of pilot season, and I had put on a bit of weight. It wasn't horrendous; most people wouldn't really have noticed. But it was the kind of thing that makes you invisible in L.A. My agent at the time claimed she could eyeball a person's weight within two ounces.

"You've gained eight pounds, *three* ounces," she told me when I went in to deliver more head shots and résumés. Pretty impressive. She could have worked at a carnival.

"Seven pounds is a size, you know."

I didn't know that, actually.

"I'm on the phone with casting people, and I'm getting lotsa '*too fat*' feedback, and you've got *carb face*."

I nodded solemnly.

"Do Atkins. That and fen-phen. Maybe throw in a colonic or two. Here—" she flipped through her massive Rolodex, scribbled something down, then handed me a slip of paper. "Call this doctor. He'll get you started."

A few hours later, I was holding a fen-phen script. I started the diet and made an appointment for a series of colonics where every other day a withdrawn woman named Daisy would shove a tube of warm water up my ass in her office in Culver City. For an hour, we'd stare at a screen in a partially darkened room watching my insides float by, Daisy, totally deadpan, announcing things like "There's an old carrot . . ."

After my "irrigation" was complete, Daisy would update my chart methodically while I put my clothes back on in the bathroom. I felt disgusting. I never felt energized the way other people claim they do following a good colonic; I just felt sad. And gross. But I would try to convince myself that I felt better, lighter, clearer, before writing the diffident Daisy a check and scheduling my next appointment.

"*Carb* face?" T.J. muttered as we pulled into the Rexall parking lot.

"Yeah. It's when your face looks all puffy from eating pasta and stuff. Think Alec Baldwin."

"He got that from spaghetti?"

"Or penne . . ."

"Hmph," T.J. fiddled with the air-conditioning.

"Anyway, this is some crazy diet," I told him. "It's all protein all the time. I eat meat, meat, and more meat. Everything you thought was bad is good, and everything you thought was good is bad. Bacon, cream, eggs, cheese—all good. Apples, bad."

"Apples are bad?"

"The worst."

"I eat them every day!"

"Well, they're terrible for you."

"Says who?"

"Says Dr. Atkins. It's all right here in his book, *Dr. Atkins' Diet Revolution*," I held up the book like they do on soup commercials.

"It's a *revolution*?"

"Damn right. I lost six fucking pounds in a week."

"So what is that, another two pounds to go?"

"Yup. And three ounces."

"And three ounces," T.J. repeated.

I explained to T.J. that as part of the whole Atkins thing, I needed these little strips that diabetics pee on to test for sugar in their urine to make sure I was still depriving myself enough to keep my metabolic pendulum swinging toward *loss*.

"Once you pee on enough sticks and stay off carbs for however long, you go into ketosis, which is the Atkins holy grail, which is what I'm in. My body, at this point only subsisting on protein, has begun to metabolize stored fat, which is essentially a highfalutin way of saying that my body is eating itself."

"And that's good?"

"It's great! You should do the diet with me. Get rid of your paunch . . ."

T.J. waited in the car reading *Dr. Atkins' Diet Revolution* while I picked up my loot.

"It says here that after you get past the two-week induction phase, you can eat macadamia nuts and drink booze," he announced cheerfully as I slid into the passenger seat.

"There's also a hotline you can call and speak to an Atkins specialist twenty-four hours a day if you're freaking out," I said.

"Hmmm," T.J. nodded, examining his pencil-thin mustache in the rearview mirror. "I think I will join you on this diet, Nahn-cee." For some reason, T.J. liked to say my name theatrically, as though he were David Niven on holiday. "But I'm starting post–induction phase so I can enjoy cocktails. How many carbs do you think are in Tanqueray?"

"I dunno. But Liz Taylor and Richard Burton once went on an all-booze diet together."

"What did they lose?"

"Their livers."

T.J. snorted.

"Well, that's gotta be at *least* a size!"

We made pretty good time driving east on the 10, then burning north through the desert, blasting Sammy Davis Jr. in T.J.'s Lincoln Mark VIII. It was a car more suitable for a golfing grandpa than a thirty-year-old personal assistant, but T.J. liked to live high on the hog. Upon scoring his most recent gig—personal assistant to eighties actor Judge Reinhold—he immediately walked into a car dealership and signed a five-year lease, with all the bells and whistles, slapping the whole shebang onto his heavily charged-up Visa card.

"I'm surprised your card didn't explode when they tried to run it," I said when he drove over to show me his new ride afterward.

T.J. just laughed and waved me off.

"It's fine. The Hollywood Assistant Employment Agency told me that Judge is up for several films back-to-back. I'll be *on set* with him for close to two years. There'll be overtime, lots of perks—I'll be in the pink in no time!"

Unfortunately, the "short ten-hour day," consisting of picking up homeopathic herbs, batteries, and dry cleaning all over town, then schlepping them back to Judge's cliffside cottage in the Palisades, lasted less than two months. Shockingly, Judge wasn't cast in any films after all.

"Things fell through," Judge told T.J.'s answering machine as he was firing him, summoning the same ho-hum dolefulness that had made him a star in *Fast Times at Ridgemont High*. "They went in a different direction." Then, as an afterthought, he added, "Gee, sorry, I know you just got that big car and everything," before hanging up.

T.J. was crestfallen. That night, at a 7-Eleven near his apartment where he went to pick up a hot dog and a Slurpee, he saw one of those Starscroll horoscopes they sell at the register. He bought one for his sign—Gemini—and perused it while eating his dinner in the car he could no longer afford, certain that what he was reading was kismet. Something about rebirth, travel, risk, blah, blah, blah, and T.J.—a balding Jay Gatsby with no money, delusions of grandeur, and a closet full of Tommy Hilfiger anoraks—decided that what he needed in that instant was to borrow five hundred dollars from our friend Matthew and spend Easter in Vegas at the roulette table.

"I'm feeling lucky," T.J. said a few hours into our trip. "Everything is a sign—everything!"

"Uh-huh."

I, on the other hand, was feeling cranky; the fen-phen made me dizzy.

"Hey, look!" T.J. pointed to some turbines, those white windmill-looking energy generators that dot the California freeways. "There's another sign! They rotate just like the roulette wheel! See what I mean?"

I watched the turbines spin languidly as we whipped along.

In my speedy daze, they beckoned us onward, flip-flopping back and forth between sinister and soothing, one minute looking like milky swastikas, the next like the Flying Nun's wimple.

We stopped at a Carrows near Barstow for an Atkins-friendly lunch: scrambled eggs with cheese, two cheeseburgers (NO BUNS), and a side of bacon.

"That was great," T.J. said as we got back in his boat. "I didn't miss the bread at all."

We arrived in Vegas in the early evening and found our accommodations, a dinky hotel and casino on the Strip right next to Bugsy Siegel's Flamingo Hotel. As soon as we were shown to our room, I whipped out my pee sticks for a quick carb check before we hit the casino.

"Oh, no!" I cried out to T.J., who was unpacking his pastel Brooks Brothers seersucker suits, which had been painstakingly wrapped in tissue to avoid wrinkling. "I'm out of ketosis! The pee stick is supposed to turn purple. It's *beige*!"

"Shall I phone Dr. Atkins?"

"T.J., this is no joke. I have no idea what happened! I was in ketosis when we left and now—"

"All right, all right, calm down," T.J. said, picking up the phone. He was able to get an Atkins specialist on the phone—some lady all the way in D.C.—and after thirty minutes of tense analysis, I was off the ledge.

"So she just thinks the extra cheese at lunch threw you outta whack, huh?" T.J. asked as we rode the elevator down to the casino.

"I should be back in ketosis in no time."

"Phew," he said. "Glad that's figured out."

"She even said I could have a cocktail or two!"

"The first Seven and Seven is on me," T.J. said, pulling out his wallet to buy chips.

We stayed down at the casino playing blackjack (me) and roulette (T.J.) and drinking cocktails until almost dawn. By that time, I was up by sixty bucks, and T.J. was down by over two hundred. My gambling edict is pretty simple: number one, I only play blackjack, and number two, I bring a hundred dollars. If I lose it, that's that. I'm done. If I'm up and lose more than two rounds in a row, I cash out. Following these rules, I usually depart gambling sojourns with winnings, unlike those who are up squillions, keep on gambling until what was won is lost, then with barely a shrug rationalize it all by saying, "I didn't *really* have that money anyway!" I am forever baffled by this: they *would* have had the money, had they *stopped*. I was with such a person on this particular Vegas excursion. T.J. would go on to lose the entire five hundred dollars he borrowed from Matthew, as well as an additional hundred he borrowed later from me. But that first night, he was still in a sanguine froth about "signs," and even losing two hundred dollars couldn't quell his chipper mood. After we cashed in my chips, we went to the coffee shop and had our free breakfast of eggs and bacon (HOLD THE TOAST, OJ, AND HOME FRIES, PLEASE!), then went to bed. Sometime in the afternoon, we woke, showered, got dressed, and, of course, I peed on a stick.

"I dunno what I'm doing wrong," I fumed to T.J. "It's *still* beige!"

T.J. got another Atkins specialist on the phone, this time some guy in Green Bay, Wisconsin. After some frantic troubleshooting, he informed me that even though the stick wasn't turning purple, I might, in fact, still be in ketosis.

"Seriously?"

"I've seen it before," Green Bay said. "Problem could be with your urine just not being particularly *potent*, thus not having the possibility of *color spectrum*, you know?"

Buoyed by this latest epiphany, T.J. and I headed to the casino coffee shop and had dinner (ROAST CHICKEN; SIDE OF SAUSAGE), then walked around Caesar's Palace. We gambled there for a bit; T.J. lost the rest of the five hundred he had borrowed, then decided that as a way of "regrouping," he wanted to explore "Gay Vegas." I was too hungry and tweaked out on the fen-phen to sleep, so I decided to join him. We drove to the edge of town and there discovered one of the most truly marvelous establishments on the face of the earth: a Western-saloon-motif discotheque, bedecked with an enormous rhinestone cowboy boot and disco ball suspended over an immaculate dance floor. Bette Midler was in Sensurround, rainbows and glitter abounded, and posters for rodeos sponsored by the International Gay Rodeo Association (and Budweiser) adorned the walls. There were gay cowboys everywhere. If hetero Vegas attracts a wholly disparate group of visitors who wander around disconnected from one another, gay Vegas is where yin and yang blend to create one totally perfect entity: masculine and feminine, the ridiculous and the sublime, highbrow and lowbrow, deconstructed, then all rolled up into the most perfect bar scene ever. *Urban Cowboy* meets *Looking for Mr. Goodbar* with a soupçon of *Star Wars*.

"I think we've arrived at the pearly gates, Nahn-cee," T.J. said as we made our way up to the bar. The cowboys all nodded to us as we passed, tipping their hats mischievously. We loitered by the bar, sipping our cocktails, and a cowboy across the dance floor started to make his way toward us.

"Look at that one, high noon, T.J.," I hissed. "He looks like he means business."

"Oh, but how I would love for him to pistol-whip me . . ."

He was very blond, wearing chaps, boots with spurs, and a red flannel shirt. His jeans were tight and faded at the crotch.

"Aloha," he said, then introduced himself. Though he dressed like a cowboy, he talked like a surfer, freely throwing around terms like "gnarly" and "rad" without the slightest irony. He was drunk and launched into a rather convoluted tale about a recent altercation he had had with some person whom he kept referring to as a "smogbreather," a surf-slur for an inhabitant of L.A. who doesn't ride the waves.

"I was, loik, totally *stoked* to be done with the *smogbreather*," the Cowboy slurred. "Dude was, loik, nothing but a *hater* with a nasty *swamp-donkey* girlfriend. It wuhn't *righteous*, wuhn't *righteous* at all . . ."

"Wow," T.J. said.

"That totally blows," I concurred, trying to be a good hag for T.J., who was clearly in the throes of new love.

"Mahalo," effused the Cowboy, winking at T.J. Then turning to me, he asked, "You seem like yur a *salty sister*. Are ya?"

"She's salty, all right," T.J. said, chortling. "You should have heard her swearing at the Atkins lady in D.C.!"

The Cowboy looked confused, but nothing was going to ruin his good vibrations.

"Most excellent!" he settled on finally.

We hung out with the Cowboy for a while, hearing stories about gnarly waves and tubular sunsets, and pretty soon he and T.J. were giving each other loving back rubs. An announcement came over the PA: a *Family Feud*–type contest was about to begin for a cash prize of five hundred dollars, the exact amount T.J. had lost so far. Three contestants were needed to make up the other "family."

"It's a sign!" T.J. said.

"*Rad sweet*, dudes! *Ka-ching!*" the Cowboy said.

"Why not?" I said.

T.J., the Cowboy, and I went up against three other random cowboys, and we almost won, until the final, fatal round. The category was "Songs about Suicide." I honestly thought we had this thing in the bag. We had "Stoney End" and "Fire and Rain" and just needed one more.

" 'It Never Rains in Southern California!' " I said, jumping up and down in our "family conference." "It's a slam dunk, you guys!"

"Naw, let's go with 'Midnight Train to Georgia,' " the Cowboy drawled. "It's a much better one."

"What the hell are you talking about?" I demanded. "How the fuck is 'Midnight Train to Georgia' about suicide, huh?"

"Isn't it just that he wasn't doing so well in L.A. so he moved back to Georgia?" T.J. asked distractedly; he was more interested in playing with the Cowboy's shirt buttons.

" 'L.A., proved too much for the man,' " the Cowboy started singing and slow dancing with T.J., who in full-blown Pip mode added the rejoinder "too much for the man."

"Yes. I realize it was *too much for him*. But he didn't kill himself," I insisted. "He just bought a one-way ticket back to the life he once knew!"

"Get it?" the Cowboy said. "*One-way ticket?*"

"It's a euphemism?" T.J. asked, scrunching up his nose.

"Of course it's not!" I screamed. "Are you an idiot?!"

"Hey!" The Cowboy was not pleased. "Maybe yur a *swamp donkey* after all!"

Our time was up, and the Cowboy answered with what was surely the dumbest answer in the history of dumb answers; the other team offered up "Theme from M*A*S*H" and won.

"I can't believe you let him give that cockamamie answer," I said as we drove back to our hotel.

T.J. just shrugged. "You didn't have to be so nasty to him."

"What kind of dope thinks 'Midnight Train to Georgia' is about suicide?"

"Well, you didn't have to be such a bitch. You've been acting just terribly since you started all this dieting."

It was true; I felt crazy.

"Well, I'm sorry," I said, petulantly. "I mean . . . I mean . . . oh, I don't know what I mean!" I screamed. "I am so fucking sick of this! Sick to death! I can't take it anymore!"

"What is the matter? Calm down!" T.J. pulled over as my hysteria mounted.

"I'm a mess, T.J. A booze-swilling, pill-popping, overweight, out-of-work mess with carb face."

I rolled down the window and lit a cig.

"I don't even know what I'm doing here, you know?"

"You mean—in Vegas?"

"Yes. No, I mean in L.A. I mean, seriously, what am I doing with my life? I don't even know anymore. I mean, I was trying to do 'art,' you know? Trying to do 'art,' whatever the fuck that is, and somehow I got stuck on this wild-goose chase where I'm, like, willing to do all this crazy crap, 'cause then, THEN, I can go back to New York, and I'll suddenly be allowed to do 'art.' But it's just absurd because I honestly don't see how doing shit turns into 'art,' and who knows, maybe 'art' is actually shit, too, and I'm just so fucked up now, T.J.! All I ever wanted— ever—was to be an actor. My whole life. What the hell happened, huh? You know, when I was little, you know, I fucking *loooved* TV, loved it like a best friend. I mean, *Match Game*? Like, where would I even be if I couldn't get that fuzzy feeling all over watching Brett Somers and Charles Nelson Reilly and . . . you know? Was that not 'art'? In some way? I mean, I felt something, you know? *I felt.* What the hell is 'art,' anyway?

Who makes the decisions, huh? Who? I got all turned around, T.J., all fucked up. I'm out here, trying to get TV work, but do I even *want* to be on TV? Maybe I do! Maybe that's the whole problem. Maybe, you know, if I get real, real honest, I did kind of deep down want to be one of those women: Lucy or Rhoda or Mary or Marilu Henner or Bonnie Franklin or Linda Lavin. Well, maybe not Bonnie Franklin or Linda Lavin, 'cause those two always bugged me—you can totally tell they're just nightmares, too—but, you know, Valerie Bertinelli or Joyce DeWitt—"

"Gawd. Remember how Joyce DeWitt came back in season two newly svelte with all the eyeliner and Liza hair?" T.J. said, grinning.

". . . or Donna Pescow! Maybe I wanted to be Donna Pescow!" I cried.

"Oh, god," T.J. said. "You mean . . . 'Angie'?"

I nodded.

"And her boyfriend was that dreamy Robert Hays . . ."

"Have my own show, you know? With a catchy opening montage, like the old ones, where the camera pans over blah-di-blue city, zooming in on the various tourist spots, the places that make you go, aha, it's Houston, or, well, clearly this is San Francisco—"

"Or Baltimore. I'd love it if you were from Baltimore—"

"And I'd be a waitress, of course."

"Of course."

"And in that same opening, there'd be glimpses of the high jinks in store, the most hilarious of which would be when I have that ubiquitous mishap with the whipped cream dispenser, and it sprays everywhere—"

"Because that happens all the time!"

"Just like in *Angie*, remember? But you know the thing

about *Angie?*" I asked, finally seeing the light at the end of the tantrum.

"That it had a dynamite theme song?"

"No. That Donna Pescow, if she was trying to be on TV today, would be considered too fat and too ugly. She'd have to lose weight and do her nose and then maybe, *maybe* . . . but even then I doubt it. There could be no *Angie* today, T.J. And what does that say?"

I started crying again. T.J. put his arm around me, gently rubbing my arm. The sky was cotton candy pink with streaks of butterscotch; Easter Sunday's dawn was erupting, and the twinkly lights of Vegas looked like neon-colored sprinkles, momentarily washing away the seediness, making Sin City look young, almost innocent.

"Well," T.J. said finally, "you're not Angie and you're not Donna. You're Nancy. And you're here because, well . . . you're here just to . . ." T.J. searched for the right word.

"Just to try," he said finally. "Just to try and, you know, do the best you can."

"Oh, god. My father used to say 'Just do the best you can' before I took tests, but I always felt that meant that he knew I was too stupid to get an A, so he was preparing me—and I guess himself—for the worst."

"Well, I meant it less literally, Nahn-cee."

"You're right. I know, you're right," I said, fishing for a Kleenex in my bag. "I just don't know how I got so far away from who I thought I was."

T.J. sighed deeply and thought for a minute. "'Funny how your feet in dreams never touch the earth.'"

"Beautiful," I said softly, blowing my nose. "Is that Tennyson?"

"No, Nahn-cee. It's Heart."

"Oh, god, of course! I love Heart!"

"Who doesn't? And I think it's fair to say that what we *need* is more Heart in this world. Less heartache, and much, much more Heart."

I nodded in emphatic agreement.

"I love you, T.J.," I said, pulling him close.

"I love you too, Nahn-cee." T.J. held my face in his hands so that our noses were touching. "And you're gonna be OK. I promise. We both are." He kissed me on the forehead, then started up the car. "Come on, it's Easter. New beginnings . . ."

Back at our hotel, we indulged in our free Easter breakfast (Denver omelets with extra cheese; bacon and sausage; NO HOMEFRIES, NO TOAST, NO OJ, YES, WE'LL HAVE THE CHAMPAGNE—WHAT THE HELL, IT'S EASTER!). I lent T.J. a hundred dollars to play roulette and went upstairs to our room to check my pee. It was still more or less beige, but like the morning sky, it had a vague pinkish tint to it. I knew I couldn't keep this up, and almost didn't care anymore, but I was lonely and decided to call an Atkins Specialist. This one was situated in New York City, a lady on the Upper East Side. Didn't she have anything better to do on Easter Sunday, I wondered, than to talk to some dumb eating-disordered actor in her fleabag hotel room in Vegas? She rattled off an erudite explanation about my pee, the details of which I can't remember. Sliding down between the twin beds in our hotel room onto the faded wall-to-wall carpet, listening to her talk, I imagined flying through the phone into Upper East Side Lady's apartment. I imagined her in some comfortable postwar place off Third Avenue in the seventies, the kind of place that had gone co-op in the late sixties, and she had gotten an insider price on it. Maybe it was a junior four with a small dining alcove done in pleasant shades of cream and robin's egg blue. I imagined that she had a small dog—a pug or possibly a Boston terrier—something not too terribly yappy but a good companion in the lonely city. After her conversation with me, she might have a walk in the park, then catch the tail end of the Easter Parade before heading over to some friends' place for a festive lamb dinner. There would be mint jelly; there would be asparagus. There would be fake grass and too much to drink and laughter.

I engaged her for a good half hour asking questions I either knew the answers to or didn't care about just so I could keep her there. As UES Lady's words spun together like slot machine lemons, I conducted an imaginary conversation with her in the spaces between my fake queries.

*Should I cut my losses and move back to New York?*

*Dieting is exhausting; I think I had more energy when I just used to starve myself.*

*There is a lyric in Lisa Loeb's song "Stay (I Missed You)" that goes, "Some of us hover when we weep for the other who was dying since the day they were born." What, exactly, does this mean?*

*What's your take on Donna Pescow?*

*What is art?*

"Lay off the nuts," she told me finally as I came out of my reverie. "The road to hell is paved with 'em." She was talking about the diet, of course. Or was she? I thanked UES Lady for her time, bade her a Happy Easter, and fell asleep for a long nap. When I woke, it was night and T.J. was sitting on the edge of his bed, removing his white bucks.

"Well, I lost," he said, then flopped back on the bed, staring up at the ceiling.

"I'm sorry, T.J."

There we were, T.J. and I, as we had been so many times before: in limbo.

We were hungry and opted for the more upscale restaurant on the premises in order to partake of the Two for One Surf 'n' Turf offer.

"Dontcha need to check your pee?" T.J. asked before we left the room.

"No," I said, picking the pee sticks up off the basin and tossing them in the toilet. "I'm all peed out."

The Surf N' Turf was excellent (EXTRA DRAWN BUTTER; HOLD THE COCKTAIL SAUCE, PLEASE!). After dinner, we took our movable feast to the casino, where I sat at the black-jack table and had a remarkable winning streak, bringing my grand total to $640. I would leave a winner.

We left Vegas the next morning and spent the long drive back listening to Sammy Davis Jr. and plotting our mutual resurrections. The moment I got home, I stepped on the scale. I had gained three pounds. I decided to simply starve myself from now on; it was easier, not to mention cheaper.

T.J. called later that evening. He had some good news.

"That Atkins stuff gets pretty fast action," he told me. "I just stepped off the scale. Would you believe I lost five pounds since Friday?"

Of course I believed it. T.J. and I both got to leave Vegas as winners, and why not? After all that we'd been through, we deserved at least that. Anyway, it's not whether you win or lose; it's how you play the game. And it helps, of course, to have a whole lotta Heart.

## 10. Take Fountain

**There was an** actor I was close to during my years in L.A., a smart, funny, sexy, cool, wildly entertaining "blond bombshell" named Gigi. She was a total throwback to a time when women were women: big hips, real tits, and unapologetically complicated. In an era like the forties, Gigi easily would have been a star, playing cynical noir sexpots like Veronica Lake in *This Gun for Hire*, or Bacall-ish heroines who needed only lower a chin or arch a brow to relay a monologue's worth of innuendo. The rub, of course, was that it wasn't the forties (it wasn't even the seventies, when the forties were "in"). It was the grunge-infested, slacker-strewn nineties, when everything, it seemed, reeked of "teen spirit," a time when heroines weren't chic, *heroin* was, and frankly, the only thing even remotely fortyish was Gigi.

We met at a party in Beachwood Canyon right about the time I made the decision to give the whole L.A. thing a go. I was with my friend Monty, who had left New York a few years before and was now happily living in one of those sweet, turreted apartments off Melrose that Charlie Chaplin had built at the dawn of Hollywood for his assorted chippies. Monty and I had spent the early part of the afternoon concocting a theory we would come to rehash for years: that it was virtually impossible to find eggs Benedict made properly (i.e., poached egg, English muffin, Canadian bacon, hollandaise sauce) anywhere in Los Angeles. We had been to four different places in the span of three and a half hours, ordering in each establishment what purported to be "eggs Benedict," and not a single one came out assembled properly. Either they did something weird like using prosciutto instead of Canadian bacon, or they fucked with the bread component, forgoing the English muffin in favor of something fancy, like a brioche or a croissant. Our servers always inquired if we would prefer our hollandaise "on the side."

New to town, I was dumbfounded. Monty tried to explain.

"It's insecurity," he hypothesized. "Out here, the baroque is fetishized, and so even breakfast is ruined."

Reeling from both our smug East Coast elitism and a woefully misbegotten bread-to-protein ratio, we decided to cool our heels and stop at a house party, a late-afternoon affair hosted by a girl we had known back in New York in the eighties when we all used to work in nightclubs. The house—one of those glorious 1920s Spanish hacienda types with a terra-cotta roof and sweeping archways—was perched on a cliff near the Hollywood sign. Billie Holiday wailed lazily, silvery curls of Nag Champa perfumed the air, and diaphanous buttercup yellow curtains billowed in and out of the three Moorish archways leading to the back loggia, where the party was in full swing. The mood was festive; everyone was imbibing either a tequila-champagne cocktail called a Hotel California, a whey protein shake made with organic bananas and magic mushrooms, or both.

I was standing in the living room talking to the hostess for a few minutes when, as if on cue, the curtains blew open to reveal Gigi, sitting at a round table of revelers beneath a sun umbrella. She wore a wide-brimmed straw hat and deep red lipstick and chain-smoked black cigarettes, which she pulled from a gold case, then lit with a Zippo, flipping it open and closed fataleishly. Gigi was one of those women who had *props*. Nothing— in her home or her handbag—was arbitrary. In this group, mostly latter-day hippies, she seemed a bit out of place: anachronistic, but not uncomfortably so. Like Kit Moresby in *The Sheltering Sky*, she was not a tourist but a traveler; home was wherever she was. I found myself inexplicably drawn to Gigi, as though I had met her a long time ago. She regarded me warily at first, but something in her jade, feline eyes told me she knew me too.

"Any advice for a new actor in town?" I asked after we were introduced.

Quoting Bette Davis, who had once been queried similarly, she replied, jokingly, "Yes: take Fountain," referring to the more easily traversed avenue that runs parallel to Sunset Boulevard.

There was a hint of expectancy tinged with neediness in how quickly Gigi's gaze morphed from vague contempt to utter helplessness, as though in spite of herself and her preconceptions, she wanted to know if I had any answers. In time, it would be revealed that she had just been through a crushing breakup with a man she adored who had traded her in for a younger model. The Beachwood Canyon party had been Gigi's first venture out in weeks. Still, breakup misery aside, I wondered about the momentary death-stare she had shot me and asked her about it months later, after our friendship was on firm footing.

"I thought you might be *her*," she said, referring to the girl she'd been dumped for. "You look like her." Then, after a beat, she sighed heavily, exhaling the smoke from one of her fancy cigarettes.

"Well, actually, she looked like *me*, if I was fifteen years younger, which is to say, she looks like *you*."

This wasn't exactly true; Gigi and I didn't really resemble each other at all. But I knew what she meant; it was more of a tribal similarity than anything in actuality, and perhaps a cosmic alignment that we shared as Librans, constantly in search of balance.

There hadn't been a great deal of balance in Gigi's life, which was perhaps why she pursued it so doggedly. As she approached her fortieth birthday, it became clear that hers was a life of extremes, with nothing turning out as expected. For one thing, the major acting career her instructors in drama school had predicted had evaded her. She arrived in New York immediately after graduation and snagged a big, juicy role in a Joe Papp production at the Public that everyone thought would move to Broadway, as *A Chorus Line* had done the previous year. The reviews were mixed, but Gigi's debut was called "incendiary," and thus buoyed, she signed a lease on a West Village flat where Edna St. Vincent Millay had supposedly once lived, and she set about buying the latest luxe-boho Talitha Getty–style frocks. Then the show closed early, never making it to Broadway; Gigi had to break her lease and sell the Talitha Getty stuff to her sister-in-law in Westchester. She became a squatter—one of six—in a walk-up loft in skeevy, ungentrified SoHo and took a job in the coat check of the Russian Tea Room. There were other acting jobs: a regional thing that looked like it might come into town but then didn't, a workshop of a new play with Mike Nichols "attached" that never went anywhere. Gigi chugged along like this for several years, excited and exhilarated by the prospect of the "big break" and then momentarily crushed when it all went inevitably up in smoke. One night while coat-checking at the Tea Room, she met a movie star's wife who took a shine to her and suggested to her husband that he help Gigi out: Wasn't there a small role in his next thing? Could he put in a word, etc.? Sure enough, a week later, Gigi was on a plane headed for L.A. and her first part in a movie.

"I wanted to make it to Hollywood before I was thirty," she told me. "And I did—barely, but still . . ."

She finished shooting her one scene on her thirtieth birthday and thought this was an omen that she was well on her way. The movie star set her up with a meeting with his agent, and after Gigi agreed to lose twenty pounds, the agent agreed to send her out on a trial basis. Gigi wasn't much of a dieter: she loved whole milk in her cereal and coffee; she adored slathering butter on thick pieces of homemade bread; she thought salad was divine, but only if it was a prelude to a steaming bowl of spaghetti carbonara or a juicy duck à l'orange. But while she might have been hungry for those delicacies, she was hungrier to realize her acting dream, so she starved herself, subsisting on espresso, sashimi, vodka, and cigarettes until she lost twenty-five pounds. But then the agent told her that her thinner face made her nose look enormous—she'd have to "do something" about it if he was to make any headway—and as if that wasn't bad enough, he announced that her scene in the movie had been cut. Gigi was shattered, but couldn't bring herself to visit the surgeon whose card the agent had pressed into her hand before sending her on her way. Soon, the agent stopped taking her calls, and then soon after that, he dropped her. Determined more than ever to succeed, Gigi called the movie star, who in turn made some calls on her behalf. She got another agent and joined a small theater company by the beach, with whom she performed classics to half-full houses four nights a week. Everyone who ever saw her in anything thought she was brilliant; everyone was positive that it was only a matter of time.

"That was ten years ago," Gigi smiled mirthlessly.

In the interim, Gigi went back to butter and whole milk ("At least I got my boobs back!"), got a job in a high-end dress shop, and had two long-term relationships with men end badly, for which she blamed herself, despite the fact that both men were horrible cads and emotionally abusive. Peppered throughout was the occasional meaty acting gig that carried with it great hope, only to slow-fade into the next scene, where the wait would begin anew.

Gigi kept the starkness of her reality, however, at arm's length. To some degree, all actors make a silent pact with themselves to never look too-too closely at their progress (or lack thereof), because if they did, they would spontaneously combust. But Gigi simply refused to examine her career at all.

Aside from my relating to Gigi's early promise and the subsequent disappointing "almosts," there was another place where we met up spiritually: in the realm of men who had left us. Whatever their unavailability or shortcomings, we felt largely responsible for their departures, as though it were owing to some inherent weakness or flaw of ours that we were left, as though these desertions were something preordained that we deserved, no matter what. Both of us had subjugated ourselves in our major romantic relationships, so much so that there was almost a sense that, like junkies out using, we had lost whole chunks of time putting ourselves and our careers on hold as we ministered to the particulars of these unions. When our men walked away, there would be great mourning periods, followed by fruitless attempts to "figure it all out," until ultimately we would return to the business of the careers we had been so passionate about until love had entered our lives. When Gigi and I met, we would have endless conversations over oolong tea on her tiny porch with the lopsided rattan furniture about our shared pathology, and why it was that two seemingly independent, sisters-doing-it-for-themselves types like ourselves could blow it all off for the sake of companionship and a good lay. We would sit smoking cigs, drinking our tea, and musing until Gigi would say, brightening, "Well, as Viola says in *Twelfth Night*, 'tis too hard a knot for me t'untie.' "

The pain etched into Gigi's face belied the flippancy and swiftness with which she could dispatch these sobering conversations, and I wondered if the theme of "undeserving" that coursed through her psyche relationship-wise extended to her stagnated career. I also always marveled at how *grand* she was, how fabulous and magnetic. She must have had a bazillion friends all over the world; she was one of those people one wanted not only to be with but *to be*. She had an uncanny ability to nutshell anyone else's issues, and for someone given to so little self-reflection, she could be remarkably insightful.

"Someone must have once told you to 'be nice,' " she said to me. "And I think you took it far too literally."

With the opposite sex, I generally found her to be strangely old-fashioned—mawkish, even. She always used the expression "so-and-so married well," which completely grossed me out, yet abhorrent though they were, there was always a kernel of truth in her pronouncements, some of which I would gnaw on for years.

"Men always reveal themselves," she told me the morning after I ended yet another terrible relationship. "They will always tell you what their *thing* is—the *thing* that will make the relationship impossible—and they'll do it on the very first date." As she paused for a second to light another cigarette, six emotions flickered across her face: innocence, rapture, wanton desire, sorrow, resignation, and grit. It was like watching the life of a woman in a time lapse.

"So," she said, exhaling smoke, "we must make an oath, you

and me: we have to pay attention. Imagine all the time we'd save if we did?"

At the time I met Gigi, she was contemplating a move to New York. L.A. was losing its luster now that her work prospects seemed to be drying up. Dumped by her man, considered by Hollywood to be just another zaftig dame, over the hill by two decades, Gigi was being pushed to the mat. Her friends knew it, her family knew it, even her dry cleaner knew the reality that was chasing Gigi, as ferociously as a pack of hounds pursuing a fox: her career wasn't working out. The parade had most likely passed her by. But Gigi didn't "go there." Maybe after one too many vodka gimlets over at Hal's in Venice she'd get depressed for a minute; it would occur to her that everyone she was friends with either was ridiculously famous or had moved on, out of the business, to other careers and houses and families. Only then, as she made her impaired way back to her tiny Silverlake apartment, would the regret and sorrow sink in. And as Tom Petty's ode to casual cruelty, "Free Fallin'," washed over her from her beyond-her-means car stereo, only then could she weep for all that she wasn't. But it was only a smidgen of grief and only for a moment; the next day, Gigi would brush herself off, throw back the curtains, and face the day once more. She could never imagine throwing in the towel even if it appeared to others to be a lost cause, because always, just as suddenly as the wave of wretchedness would rise, the call would come: a job, out of nowhere, the flicker of potential that invariably made her stay at the fair. Yes, it was always something small—so small you could blink and miss it—but it was *something*: something to say when asked the inevitable "What are you up to these days?," something that Gigi could dine out on for weeks. "You see," she would say, wiping a relieved tear away from her eye, to her concerned but undermine-y sister, who had called from her suburban hell to plead with Gigi yet again to have the baby before it was too late, "I'm still in it."

There were many days when I would watch her puttering around her tiny living room in her silk kimono, phone in the crook of her neck, cigarette ablaze, chattering away to this friend or that. Hers was a life, it seemed, lived on a perpetual call-waiting, clicking on and off, on and off. "Soon," she'd purr as her sign-off, not 'bye, or ciao, or later, but "soon," because it was so optimistic, so much more future-looking. Sitting there, marveling at the choreography it took to be this stunning creature, I would wonder how different this day, this scene, looked from virtually every other day of her life over the past ten years. Winter looked essentially no different from summer in L.A., so if you really wanted to, you could convince yourself you had only just arrived. I could never fathom how Gigi kept going, what tricks she used on herself, what mantras she repeated. As much as I admired and adored her, envied her talent, her wit, her style, her magical aura, at the same time my biggest nightmare was that I would one day become her: still struggling, acting less and less, and ignoring that reality more and more. I could think of no worse fate, nothing scarier. Like my very own Dorian Gray, come to life, out of the attic, thrust under my nose. Watching her rationalizing, plotting, dragging her car with the fucked carburetor for the umpteenth time to the mechanic in Hollywood (the one who always gave down-on-their-luck actresses a break, charging them little or nothing at all, depending on how low their resources or cleavage-revealing necklines), agonizing over credit card debt brought on by a terrifying Barneys bender—I would become bitter *for* her, asking myself, "When, when does one know it's time to stop?"

\* \* \*

Gigi finally made the decision to switch coasts during my rainy first winter living in the Hollywood Hills. We kept in touch on the phone and occasionally through wacky cards we'd stuff with a single dollar bill and the encouragement via PS to "buy something pretty!"

A year or so later, my own career at an impasse, I was lying deflated one morning in my Fairfax apartment staring blankly at the cottage cheese ceiling. I was late with the rent; there was an eviction notice on my door, and I was resorting to selling my clothes for cash with my friend Kate on the sidewalk in front of my building later that day. The phone rang, and I let the machine pick it up.

"I got a job," Gigi choked through tears. "On Broadway . . ."

I immediately picked up the phone, and as she recounted the story of landing what would be her Broadway debut at the age of forty-five, I wept along with her.

"Oh my god, Gigi," I cried. "You did it. You really, really did it!"

"I know," she whispered. "I know."

She got great reviews; there was talk of London, a movie. But then the job ended and . . . nothing. It didn't change a thing. Gigi went back to the shit job she had at some store and sat stunned in front of the register each day, from eleven to seven, like a bird who's flown into a window but doesn't die.

Eventually, she made her way back to L.A. Her old landlord gave her back her old pad; her old boss gave her back her old gig at the high-end dress shop. It was almost as though she had never left at all. In fact, the only thing that reflected the truth—that time had not simply stood still—was Gigi's face. It wasn't lines, though she had a few of those, around her eyes mostly, a few around her mouth vaguely discernible when she fired up one of her fancy smokes. It was far more dramatic: her face had begun to droop since the last major disappointment, and though still as bewitching and glamorous as ever, her mask bore the unmistakable weight of a life's worth of chagrin. Like a soufflé perturbed by a loud sound or an overanxious cook, Gigi's face had fallen from the disquiet her cheerful personality could no longer disguise.

Shortly after she arrived back in town, I had dinner one night with Gigi, whose car was once again in the shop. Dropped off at the restaurant by another friend, she arrived, as usual, in a puff of drama and perfume.

"I had a dream last night," she told me after we were settled and had started in on some pinot from the Russian River. "The strangest dream. I was riding in a parade, a ticker tape parade . . ."

She paused to think about this for a moment, pulling one of her black cigs from her gold case.

"I don't remember what happened first, you know, before that part. I only remember the ticker tape part and that I was riding through it, sitting on the back of a convertible . . ."

"Yeah."

"Anyway, so I'm riding on the back of this convertible. Everyone's smiling, waving, yelling, '*Gi-gi! Gi-gi!*,' and I'm waving back at them, so of course, in my mind, I figure I'm in a movie, you know, I'm shooting a scene in a movie."

Gigi leaned forward, her eyes widening incredulously.

"But after a while, it begins to dawn on me: This ain't no movie. This is real! And not only that, this whole damn thing is for me!" She laughed, lighting her cigarette.

"Wow—"

"Right?"

"So positive—"

"Isn't it? And *powerful*?"

"Like a flying dream—"

"It was *so* fabulous . . ."

We cracked up, taking in this image, sipping our wine for a few moments. Gigi's cheeks began to flush, and at first I thought it was the pinot, but then I saw it: her eyes welling with tears.

"What is it?" I asked, reaching for her hand.

"I don't know," she said, carefully dabbing her napkin around the corners of her eyes, trying in vain to find her reflection in her fish knife to make sure there were no delinquent mascara streaks. "It's just that . . ."

"What?"

"It was *so beautiful*, the ticker tape, you know? I—I just never noticed that before. So beautiful and . . . fun and . . . messy—" Gigi grabbed her napkin and started dabbing again, this time at fully formed tears. She composed herself for a moment, checked her makeup once again in her flatware, then smiled.

"I don't know what it was about that ticker tape," she said finally. "It seemed so hopeful, yet something about it makes me feel so sad."

"Were you happy in the dream?"

"I think so," Gigi began slowly, then stopped to think. "I was. I know I was," she decided finally. "I guess I just wasn't able to fully embrace it because by the time I realized it was real and for me, it was over."

"Isn't it always that way?"

"And that's what feels so sad. By the time I figured it out, it was over."

After dinner, I gave Gigi a lift home. Sunset was, as usual, a nightmare.

"Swing down to Fountain," she said. "It's always a breeze."

But Fountain, too, was a snarled, trafficky mess.

I looked ahead into the midnight blue, dotted with headlights and the occasional red glow of brakes, and thought back to that Beachwood party and my first conversation with Gigi, when she so blithely tossed off the "Take Fountain" suggestion. It was a joke, of course; she was just repeating some Bette Davis shtick for the benefit of the film queens she was in the company of, but I would soon come to see that she also meant it in earnest. How many times had I heard her say—to me and to other friends—"Oh, take Fountain. It'll be a breeze"? And the thing is, it *never was*. It was always just as bad as any other street in L.A. Maybe back in the days when people like Bette Davis roamed the earth, a street like Fountain was clear and open, a fabulous little shortcut that could make you feel like you were in on some secret. But now, Fountain Avenue was just another byway, crowded with hopefuls desperate to get some-where in a jiffy, only instead idling bumper to bumper, waiting, spilling oil in a holding pattern along with everyone else who thought they held the key to getting places in a hurry in L.A.

"See," Gigi said after a few minutes, "much better."

"Fountain sucks," I said. "It's always jammed."

"Is it?" Gigi asked. "Strange . . . I never noticed that."

But I didn't believe her. I think she did notice; she just never let it get to her. As with the ticker tape in her dream, or her career for that matter, Gigi noticed what she needed to notice in order to keep going. She had none of the cynicism or anger that came nat-urally to someone like me. For so long, Gigi had seemed to me such a sad—even delusional—figure, washed up and not dealing with it, like so many other wannabes. But as I drove her home that night, it dawned on me that maybe I had been wrong: maybe Gigi in fact had the right temperament to be an actor, a working actor, slogging along, with nary a negative thought, just trying to make sure to get SAG insurance for another year and maybe—maybe—get a hit here or there. Looking at her life, with all the bills, the car crap, the money issues, the bad boyfriends, the call-waiting, waiting, waiting, it was hard not to want to scream at the injustice that this woman, this enormously talented, vivacious woman, was not a huge star, rich and famous and beloved by throngs of fans unknown to her.

Maybe her definition of success was less complicated than mine, less rigid and less dependent upon conventional thought. Maybe it was enough that she was able to do what she loved, whether it brought her fame and wealth or not. Sure, she would have liked to be making her living this way, but at the least she got to do it at all, and maybe, for her, this was enough. She wasn't, after all, miserable on a daily basis—I was.

I felt terrible for how I had judged her—my friend, whom I genuinely thought the world of—how I had often shuddered lying awake at night, terrified of "becoming Gigi." It was not Gigi who needed to accept the truth of her situation, but me.

We hugged for a long time when we reached her apartment; both of us seemed to be hanging on to something more than just each other: the moment, perhaps, or maybe the memory of other moments we'd never really felt the need to say good-bye to. Wanting, I suppose, to bestow upon her some advice of my own, I offered this tidbit:

"You know, I've found that if you *really* want to get across town faster, you take Sixth. We should change the expression."

Gigi smiled and smoothed my hair.

"True," she said, getting out of the car. "But it doesn't sound as good."

## 11.  Hero-Goal-Obstacle

**For the most** part, the men I dated after the Jazz Musician generally veered between the bizarre and the abusive. There was Larry, a lawyer/wannabe actor who had failed his bar exam three times and whose mother, with whom he still lived, hated me so nakedly that whenever I arrived at his house, her eyes would glaze into limpid pools of despair. Larry was very dumb— dumbest guy I have ever dated, and also notable for being the dumbest Jewish guy I had ever known. We once got into a knock-down, drag-out fight because he refused to believe he had an unconscious.

After Larry, I went out with a stuntman I met at spinning class, who each day, from the moment we met, would bring beautiful, sweet-smelling roses from his garden and present them to me before we mounted our fake bikes. He was one of those ultra-rugged guys who made scads of money driving erratically through the Arizona desert for car commercials. It seemed apropos, then, that he should take me on my first car date in years. He picked me up one night and, after handing me a huge bouquet of homegrown dusty pink roses, whisked me off in his white, O.J.-style Bronco to dinner at Yamashiro, where we had a lovely time sharing sushi and looking at the spectacular view. I had an eight A.M. call time the next morning, so I needed to make it an early night, but after dinner, the Stuntman drove me not home but rather to his all-white modern abode in deepest Laurel Canyon. I had no idea where I was; I had thought he was taking me to my place. When I refused to leave his garage and enter the house, he finally agreed to take me home, but not before telling me that all women were skanks, opportunists, and thieves.

Then there was Neil. I met Neil at a Passover dinner at a friend's apartment in Beverly Hills. The only guy there, Neil spoke a smattering of Hebrew, so he ended up in the "dad" position, presiding over the seder for the evening, and by the time he was instructing us girls to dip our bitter herbs in the salty-tears water, I was ready to sleep with him. Neil was an actor and loitered away on episodic television, playing roles typically given to swarthy, hirsute ethnic guys: surgeons, defense lawyers, rapists—men who lived large and loved to laugh. In fact, Neil did a lot of laughing on TV. He had a big, booming laugh he could bust out at the drop of a hat, over and over when the scene required it; he was to laughing what Meryl Streep was to weeping. But in life, Neil didn't laugh much at all, especially if you were a woman. Divorced, fucked over too many times by too many broads, including (especially?) his mother, Neil thought women were the most unfunny creatures on the planet. Any of my attempts to be funny—even just lighthearted banter—were viewed with scorn and contempt. A scowl would wash across his stubbly face; he would defiantly cross his arms as if to say, "Go ahead. Just *try*." Comedy, Nautilus machines—these were for people with penises as far as Neil was concerned. The only female he was really compatible with was his large, brindled pit bull, Brenda. One day, I just stopped calling Neil back; I briefly went back to New York for a wedding, and when I returned, I just didn't call him. Soon after, I went to Adray's, this discount electronics place on Wilshire, to buy a scale and ran into Neil in the line where they check your receipts to make sure you're not stealing.

"THERE YOU ARE!" he screamed in front of dowager-humped old people buying toaster ovens and hipsters with eyebrow rings buying fans. "YOU THINK IT'S OK TO JUST NOT FUCKING CALL ME EVER AGAIN? HUH? YOU THINK THAT'S *FUNNY*? YOU'RE A ROTTEN LITTLE BITCH. FUCK YOU. FUUUUUCK YOOOOU!"

He wasn't the worst, though. That distinction goes to the Springsteen freak who told me that I reminded him of "Thunder Road" because of the lyric "You ain't a beauty but hey, you're alright, oh, and that's alright with me." Despite the aforementioned (and the fact that he was terrible—and I mean *terrible*—in bed), I slept with him for six months. And there were others, many others. I point to this mortifying stretch of my dating history merely as a way of illustrating how hideously low my self-esteem had sunk during this time. I stayed in things and with people so far past their expiration dates that I didn't notice the taste of curdle anymore because, for whatever reason, I felt inside like I deserved it. And it was so insidious, this motif of self-penalization, that it metastasized to every area of my life, including my seemingly innocuous first writing class, a sitcom-writing workshop taught by a curmudgeonly old-school TV writer.

The Curmudgeon was very well regarded; he had written and produced countless episodes of classic sixties and seventies sitcoms, and everyone raved about him. I knew a few people and had heard of others who were staffed onto big shows immediately after completing his twelve-week session. I wasn't sure I wanted to write for sitcoms—I wasn't sure I wanted to *act* on them either—but I had been wanting to take a writing class of some sort for years and thought maybe this would be a good way to get my feet wet.

The class met at the Curmudgeon's homestead, nestled into a rustic canyon in West L.A. Twelve of us—as well as the Curmudgeon and his three halitosis-hampered setter-type dogs—would sit around a conference table in the Curmudgeon's living room. The Curmudgeon had a whiteboard, onto which he had Magic Markered the words "Hero-Goal-Obstacle." This, according to the Curmudgeon, was really all you needed to know to write basically anything.

"The hero always has a goal, which is made known to us at the top," the Curmudgeon croaked, pointing to his whiteboard.

"The plot is made up of the obstacles we put in the hero's way to give *dramatic tension* while he pursues his goal. And that's it. If you don't have these things, you can forget it."

The Curmudgeon would give us scene assignments each week—all taken from his TV-writing files amassed thirty years before—which we were to complete, bring in, pass out to everyone, and cast. We were not allowed to read our own stuff; the Curmudgeon just wanted us to listen when our work was being read. The assignments always involved a very dopey premise. I remember one involved an anthropologist couple who, after having endured a lengthy work-related separation, are insanely horny for each other and desperate to fuck (Hero-Goal). The woman has schlepped a large gorilla back from the African jungle as a gift for the husband. The gorilla, as it happens, is very jealous and keeps interfering every time the husband tries to put the moves on (Obstacle).

Each time I heard one of these assignments, my first thought was "This is really stupid." But then I would get into it; I thought maybe the Curmudgeon's point was to warm us up with insipid exercises, and if we could make those funny, well, we could do anything—and then he would pull out the *actually* funny stuff that we might get hired to do. It took me several weeks to realize that . . . this was it. There was no graduating to better assignments. The Curmudgeon was adamant that if the material didn't work, it was our fault; there were no bad setups, only bad writers. Period. If you were working the Hero-Goal-Obstacle concept, there should be no issue. At first, I liked the class and the Curmudgeon, though I did feel uncomfortable that he was always very flirty with me.

"Well, hullo there, you sexy dame!" he hollered from the conference table when I walked in for the second session of the workshop. "Why dontcha come sit right next to me so I can fondle you while we listen to some screamingly funny scenes?"

In the past, I didn't take too kindly to overt displays of sexual hostility. Once, when I was in the Catskills for a season of summer theater, a guy in a pickup truck yelled something lewd to me as he passed me walking on a rickety bridge. "Fuck you, asshole!" I screamed, hurling a can of Diet Coke at his door. He screeched to a halt and vowed to slit my throat; my bucolic respite was poised to become a scene from *Deliverance*. But I was too enraged to concern myself with matters of safety; recklessness be damned. When similarly propositioned by catcalling construction workers on New York City streets, I would stop dead and scream, "Wild horses couldn't drag me anywhere near you, motherfuckers!" My blood boiled at how cheap their jeers made me feel and what I perceived as their unchecked sense of macho entitlement.

But here, not wanting, I suppose, to seem like I had no sense of humor in a comedy-writing class, I merely glanced awkwardly toward the other writers at the conference table, whose faces evinced indifference. Averting my eyes, I looked for a seat, only to discover that the only chair available was right next to the

Curmudgeon. This seating configuration was almost always the same, no matter how early or late I arrived. But I will never forget that first time: queasily sinking into my chair, the Curmudgeon grabbing my right knee, a stinky dog's snout resting on the left one, while the other two brethren lay comatose, having whimpering doggie nightmares on my feet.

A week or so later, I told my friend Gabe, who was writing for television, about the Curmudgeon's unbridled bellowing and wandering fingers, and he was fairly dry-eyed.

"Get used to it," he told me. "That kinda stuff goes on all day in the writers' room. It's a boy's club."

"Really? What about sexual harassment?"

"What about it? Television isn't the corporate world."

"I know, I know," I sighed. "It's Hollywood . . ."

"Worse; it's Burbank."

Gabe went on to say that if anyone could stomach these types of shenanigans—any "chick," that is—it was me. Historically, this had been true: rednecks and construction workers aside, it wasn't unusual for me to be cool with a little harmless objectification. I generally fared well with male rough-and-tumble, in-your-face aggressiveness; they dished it, I took it and relished throwing it right back in their faces. In the past, I had viewed it as a feather in my cap that unlike some women whose wan dispositions precluded rolling with the punches, I was a "tough cookie"; I knew how to take a joke. Besides, I had always craved male friendship, needed their attention (even if it was more of a punch than a caress). Like Anybodys in *West Side Story*, I was always desperate to be included in the gang. But by the time I enrolled in the Curmudgeon's class, things had changed; I felt different. Perhaps it was turning thirty, or because, more often than not, the camaraderie I thought I had with men came to disappointing conclusions, leaving me confused and hurt, face-to-face with the sham these bonds were really based on. Or perhaps I was just really tired of always having to "take a joke" when it involved me as the sex object.

My discomfort with the Curmudgeon and my knee, however, didn't stop me from feeling enthusiastic about writing. I attacked my assignments each week with a zeal theretofore unobserved, save for the time I wrote the short one-act in David Mamet's master class back at NYU. I hadn't seen Mamet in five years at that point; the last time was at a dinner in Vermont when a friend and I were passing through. Mamet had a new house and a new wife and soon after our arrival ran around ebulliently explaining how to use the new rotisserie he had just installed in his kitchen.

"You take this pole, stick it up the chicken's fucking asshole, then it rotates on this thing. It is delicious and I am in awe . . ."

He was madly in love, discovering yoga, reclaiming his Jewish roots, and genuinely happy and at peace in a way I had never experienced him before.

"Are you writing?" he asked me later, after we cleared the plates.

"Not really," I told him. "I start things; I just don't finish them. Maybe I need to take a class or something."

He shook his head.

"How do you learn to swim?"

I shrugged.

"You get in the water."

I didn't keep in touch with Mamet after that; I felt embarrassed that I had gone to L.A. the following year with all the "whores," and more shamefaced that I had never written anything really substantial after that long-ago one-act. But he sometimes paid me visits during my L.A. years, courtesy of my imagination, as he did when I was taking the Curmudgeon's class. He would pop into the seat across from me at the kitchen table of my apartment off Fairfax, waxing reflective, phlegmatically quoting others about the perils of Hollywood, pestering me as I labored over my inane exercises.

"Hollywood is like being nowhere and talking to nobody about nothing."

"Behind the phony tinsel of Hollywood lies the real tinsel."

Sometimes I would even conjure up Mamet on my long rides west on Sunset Boulevard to the Curmudgeon's class. He would sit stoically in his baseball cap, smoking a cigar, his foot on the dash of the beat-up Volkswagen convertible I had bought used in Hermosa Beach, repeating the maxims of other men.

"Hollywood is like a trip through a sewer in a glass-bottom boat."

One day about halfway through the Curmudgeon's twelve-week session, I arrived with a scene I wanted to have read. The Curmudgeon suggested I cast another woman he flirted openly with, a very attractive commercial actor. I immediately agreed. It was always great if you could use a real actor to read scenes, and most of the people in the class were just writers. No sooner did the woman start reading, however, than I realized something was wrong. She was mangling the lines: dropping words, adding words, reading haltingly, devoid of any rhythm whatsoever.

"Whoops," she giggled, looking up momentarily. "Sorry, I'm *dyslexic . . .*"

After the scene died a slow, miserable death, the Curmudgeon started to give me notes, pointing out lines for their terribleness, which hadn't actually been lines I'd written; they were lines delivered by the actor in her dyslexic befuddlement. Normally, we were prohibited from responding to his comments, but seeing as how he was commenting on lines I had, in fact, not written, I thought it best to explain.

Immediately, the Curmudgeon exploded into a red-faced fit.

"YOU DON'T SPEAK!" he shouted, his puffy, cataracty eyes practically spinning, while his liver-spotted hands shook with rage. "YOU SIT THERE AND YOU SHUT THE FUCK UP AND YOU *LISTEN*!"

Completely horrified by his reaction, I instantly shut up, and wrote fake notes onto my version of the script as he continued his bellowing. As it started to sink in, I vacillated between wanting to flee and being completely shut down: frozen, unable to think, feel, breathe. There had been dozens of times in my past when I had found myself in the role of receptacle for a man's misplaced rage, and in those times I would simply settle into a strange, trancelike complacency. It never mattered how scary these bursts of madness were, nor how irrational; I would sit through them in a muddled paralysis, willing myself not to cry, mostly believing that *they* were *right*. That night, as I stared at the blurred type, writing dummy notes in the margins of my script, was the first time I recognized this pattern, the first time I was acutely aware of where I went in these moments. "Something about this," I thought as I sat there that night, "feels comfortable." It was a scene I knew, a scene I had played countless times, as familiar as if I had written it myself. I had always been conscious of the mixed emotions I had about being a woman, sometimes wondering in that abstract way that you do whether things would have been easier, whether, if I had been exactly me in terms of looks, personality, and talent but a guy, not a girl, I would have been easier to hire, to admire, to love. But lingering on these questions, these concerns, wasn't my thing; frankly, I found them boring. Still, something about being on the receiving end of the Curmudgeon's vituperation that night, sitting there beneath my familiar mask of apathy yet so utterly shaken to the core, made me look into the deep, dark vat of my feigned toughness and see that what it actually held was profoundly internalized shame.

I barely made it to my car before I disassembled after the Curmudgeon's class. Blinded by tears, I drove into the night, sure I would never make anything of myself, sure I was, once again, wasting my time, my money, wondering why nothing ever worked out, and feeling doomed to failure, heartbreak, and bad luck.

"Luck has nothing to do with it," my mirage Mamet told me as I sobbed. "It's not about luck; luck is an accident. You want to write; it's hard work. You want to like yourself; stop fucking hating yourself."

"Right," I said. "Like it's that fucking simple."

"It *is* that fucking simple: You have created a habit, a bad one. So change. Create a new one. A good one."

I thought about the brio I'd once had when I'd studied with Mamet and company, how confident I had been then that there was nothing I couldn't pull off. It had only been ten years since I'd graduated, and yet I could no longer summon any of the dauntlessness that had once been so easy. Maybe none of it had been real; maybe it had been merely a masquerade, a puffed-up bit of stage business with no real foundation to support it. Maybe it had been dampened somewhere along the way, snuffed out after the various plunders, the rejections, the if onlys, the almosts. Or, maybe I had, in my infinite lack of self-regard, simply frittered it all away.

"Remember," the phantom Mamet said, "if you go to hell, you shouldn't be surprised by the heat."

"What does that even mean?" I asked.

"It means that there are no easy answers and no magic

tricks. I told you before: be brave, be strong, tell the truth. It scares you? Fine. *Do it anyway.* You want to feel better about yourself? Very simple: *exercise your will.* Make a decision, then fucking stick to it. The end."

I slept for almost twenty-four hours straight following the Curmudgeon's blowup. When I awoke, I decided to schedule the visit with a psychic that my friend Kate had bought me a year and a half before as a thirtieth-birthday gift. I had wanted to "save up" for when I felt really in a psychic pickle, and there was no better time than when I was losing my mind, at the end of my tether as an actor, and getting reamed by grumpy old gropers.

A week later, I arrived for my afternoon appointment at the Oakwood Apartments in Studio City, where the psychic had a small room. I had never been to the Oakwood, though I had passed it countless times on my way to and from the Valley for auditions and jobs, but as I pulled into the visitor parking, it occurred to me that this was the very same temporary housing complex that Jane had suggested to me nearly three years before when I was in need of lodging. The lobby, resplendent in beige and fake wood veneer, was teeming with child-star hopefuls from all over the country, rehearsing auditions with their stage mothers, their bored siblings, meanwhile, plopped aimlessly on the carpet at Mama's feet, playing jacks or coloring, building up resentments for future dramas of their own. In the psychic's tiny room, for the next two hours, I listened to predictions I knew would never come true:

I would move to London.

I would have three children.

I would have problems with my feet.

In the not-so-recent past, I would have clung to the clairvoyance of strangers as though each absurdity were a decree. (To wit: Once, in the aftermath of breakup number two with the Jazz Musician, I called a psychic in Tennessee, who spoke to me in the voice of one of my ovaries. Apparently, this was where my "spirit life" was located. Wacky, yes, and even wackier that my "ovary" had a thick Southern accent, and still . . . *I believed*.) But by the time I stumbled into the Oakwood, I had long since given up thinking that these things yielded much. Driving home after the session was over, however, I had to admit that there were three things the Oakwood psychic had said that piqued my imagination: I would publish a book; I was a moment away from meeting the man I would marry; and finally, before either of these things could happen, first I had to go back to singing, something I hadn't done or even thought about in years. Why these three prophecies gave me pause when the aforementioned "foot problems" struck me as insane, I don't know; they sounded just as far-fetched as anything I had ever heard before, and yet they rolled over and over in my mind. *Singing*. I had sung as a child; it was how I had started as a performer and what had led me, ultimately, to acting. Then, once I became a "serious actor," singing became a thing of the past. For a brief while, when I was with the Jazz Musician, I took it up again, singing little gigs at the Knickerbocker in the Village, at an Italian joint in the theater district, and even at a small room in Harlem, where they paid us in smothered-chicken dinners. As much as I enjoyed it, though, by that time in my life it was really just a way to be with my boyfriend. When we broke up, I could barely listen to standards, let alone sing them, and so, when the Jazz Musician left, so too did my desire to be a chanteuse. It all felt like another lifetime ago.

Several weeks after my visit to the Oakwood psychic, we all gathered for my friend Monty's birthday party at the Dresden

Room. Everyone was there: T.J., Kate, me, and assorted others, toasting Monty and listening to the dulcet tones of the Dresden Room's Marty and Elaine, the duo immortalized in the movie *Swingers*. Marty and Elaine were generally known for singing a deranged operatic version of the sound track to *Saturday Night Fever*, but on occasion, they also invited people to sit in with them. After several rounds of drinks, Monty asked me to sing, and though it had been years since I'd done so publicly, I was just drunk enough to do it. With my friends cheering me on, I called the tune—Cole Porter's "All of You"—and though I counted off a languid tempo, Marty and Elaine only play one speed: fast. Nevertheless, it all went so well, and I received such a rousing response, that they let me sing a second tune. When I finished, I was approached by a man who offered me a job singing with his big band at the Atlas Bar and Grill. Rehearsals would begin the following month. I was excited, but I knew it was one thing to sing drunk with the spastic Marty and Elaine to an equally drunken crowd and quite another to do it professionally. I needed a piano player to rehearse with so I could get back into shape and work up my old song charts—but where?

The following week, I attended a performance of a play that Monty was understudying the lead in, and while Monty was good, the play left much to be desired. I found myself zoning out, listening to the music that punctuated the scene changes, played offstage by an unseen pianist. It was the same style of hard-bop jazz that I had heard in New York all the time, but found rarely in Los Angeles. The play, though interminable, finally came to an end, and while waiting to give Monty my congratulations, I ran into the artistic director of the theater company, whom I also knew.

"Listen," I told him, "I've got to meet that piano player. I need to hire him for something!"

At that moment, a boyish-looking guy in a suit walked through the theater doors and into the lobby, drinking a Coke.

"Here he is right now," said the artistic director. "Joel, Nancy. Nancy, Joel . . ."

After I explained what I needed to Joel, we exchanged numbers and made a plan to rehearse, which had to be put on hold for several weeks when I booked my second and third *Seinfeld* appearances. This sudden boon to my acting career resulted in the Atlas Bar and Grill job falling through, since I was unable to make it to rehearsals while I was on the other side of town on a soundstage. With no Atlas job, I no longer needed a piano player, but when I spoke to Joel on the phone, he convinced me it might be fun to work up an act of our own and see if we couldn't get any gigs. Joel knew a bass player and a drummer, and we scheduled a rehearsal session at Joel's place, a guesthouse in Beverly Hills. Rehearsal went well, so we set up another, but we also decided that I should first have some rehearsals alone with Joel so he could work out keys and arrangements for me before we reconvened en masse.

For the next few weeks, every other day, I would go over to Joel's and work on songs, dragging my big music books from the trunk of my car, past the pool on my way in, past the pool on my way out. Joel shared his guesthouse with two sickly roommates: a mangy cat named Ludwig, whose dull white fur stood up in clumps around his body (and whom Joel was nursing back to quasi health by hooking him up to an IV every few hours for re-hydration), and a near-dead houseplant named Bruce that he'd stuck in a dark closet, watering it twice a day.

"He doesn't look so good," I said when Joel first introduced me to Bruce, who tilted piteously to one side and whose brittle brown leaves were so sparse that he reminded me of Charlie Brown's Christmas tree. "I think Bruce might be dead."

"I know," Joel shrugged. "But I still figured he was worth a try . . ."

I couldn't help being charmed by Joel's attempts to save ailing kitties and fading flora; he was very cute, this self-effacing guy with the sad green eyes and the dry wit, and he had the sort of mild misanthropy about him that I had always found so fresh and appealing. In time, as we rehearsed songs about love, desire, and dreams, I found myself singing directly to the tiny bald spot that peeked out from the top of his head. I started to look forward to rehearsing with him just so I could see him, and soon I was staying longer and longer after we worked, just to tell him stories about my crazy life that would make him laugh.

After playing just one gig together, Joel and I gave up the act and started dating instead. One day, he gave me his old laptop and bought me a three-day memoir-writing workshop as a surprise. The workshop, led by a writer appropriately named Faith, was filled with about fifteen women who routinely used the word "journal" as a verb. I didn't know what to expect—certainly not much—but the workshop was amazing: informative without being patronizing, hand-holdy without being treacly. And each of the three days, I would run home and write all night long. As I read my stories—or, more accurately, fragments, snapshots, and character sketches—I looked across the circle of desks at caring, attentive faces who who seemed to know what I was talking about. Aping Mamet and horny apes were a thing of the past, and there was no reason to hide. "Tell the truth," he had said, and finally, I felt like I could.

Ten months after our first rehearsal, Joel asked me to marry him; ten months after that, in the merry month of May, we were hitched on the first day of a new moon. Ludwig died not long after our engagement; I found him, lying curled up in his litter box. As I knelt crying and petting his matted fur, I couldn't help relating to the poor soul whose life had ended in his own toilet. How often I believed my fate would be similar. We had known Ludwig wasn't long for this world, but somehow both Joel and I were completely shaken by his passing. Then, a month before our wedding, Bruce came out of the closet. He was not only alive but thriving, green and flowering. I couldn't believe it.

"How did you know?" I asked Joel as we stood marveling at the magnificent plant I had taken for dead when I'd met him.

"I just never gave up on him," Joel said.

And although I knew that Joel felt the same way about my potential as he did about Bruce's, perhaps his greatest gift to me was making me see that I had not yet given up on myself.

## 12. Beverly D'Angelo's Former Manager

**"I didn't think** it was possible," my agent said a few hours after I had blown an audition for a TV movie, "but you managed to bore Luke Perry."

Arriving in the Room for the audition, I was introduced by an assistant, then went the usual left to right down the conference table, shaking hands with the director, the casting director, and so on, and when I got to the dude in the backward baseball cap, I was stunned to discover that it was . . . ohmygod . . . *Luke Perry?* For some reason, despite the fact that this was an audition for something called *The Untitled Luke Perry Project*, this was terribly startling. I proceeded then to have a thoroughly horrible audition, reading a scene with the casting director and all the while thinking things like "Luke Perry is leaning back in his chair. Luke Perry is sucking on . . . a lollipop? A straw? A pen? Luke Perry is taking off his baseball hat, rubbing his hat-head hair (is his hairline receding?) and putting the cap back on again. Luke Perry, Luke Perry, Luke Perry (who cares?! You never even watched *90210!*) Luuuuuke Peeeeeeer-rrry."

It was very disconcerting: I was a shaking, stammering imbecile because I was thrown off guard by *Luke Fucking Perry*. How far I had fallen. Once upon a time, I would go into the

Room for an audition and knock it out of the park no matter who was there. I might not *get* the part, but I was always prepared and ready to roll, totally unfazed by the particulars. Only a few years before, I auditioned for the film *Quiz Show*. I was put on tape reading a few scenes, and later that day I received a call: you are to come back tomorrow to meet Robert Redford. Robert. Redford. *Hubbell. Gardner.* I was scared sitting in the waiting room, but Redford ("You can call me Bob") was so disarming that any fear I had evaporated. I didn't get the part, but it was a great audition and remains to this day the best I have ever had. Hubbell—I mean *Bob*—even sent me a personal letter (yes, I have it in a frame) saying how terrific I was, how *hard* it had been not to cast me. (*Oh, Hubbell! Can it be that it was all so simple then?*) So walking into the Room and seeing Luke Perry should have been a nonevent. But those days were long gone, baby. Luke Perry thought I sucked. And he was right: I did.

"Honestly," my agent said, "I really can't work with you anymore. You're too much of a loose cannon."

And just like that, I was agentless again for the first time in years. Not that my agent was so great; she hardly ever sent me out, and I was always having to hustle casting people who knew me or had hired me before. But a crappy agent, like a crappy boyfriend, always seemed better than none at all. *Someone* supposedly finds you worthwhile and adorable!

"You seem like the type *America* would like to invite into their living room," this last agent said when signing me two years before. But not, apparently, into *her* living room; I rarely heard from her, except when she would call to let me know about an audition I had procured for myself.

After my agent dropped me, I got under my covers and sobbed for a while, then, puffy-eyed and headachy, dragged myself over to my friend Monty's, to coach him for an audition.

I vowed to him, as I had after every letdown in the past, that I was quitting show business and getting my real estate license.

"Nance," Monty said, laughing, "you'd make a horrible real estate agent."

"Well, then maybe I'll start designing jewelry."

"I don't see you doing anything involving welding either . . ."

The next day, after talking it over with Joel, who was by now my husband, I decided that Monty was right; I didn't need a welding torch. All I needed was a new agent. Unfortunately, this proved to be harder than I'd thought: no one was interested in signing me. "Let me know when you're in something," they would say when I called about a meeting. Agents were always saying, "Let me know when you're in something," an update on "Don't call us, we'll call you." The thing is, you couldn't get *in something* without them *sending you out*.

"Why don't you write something for yourself to perform?" Joel said.

I hated solo shows; most were appalling and desperate, devoid of any redeeming purpose, the entire venture based solely on the actor's barely concealed cri de coeur, "GET ME AN AGENT— FAST!" But now, I *was* that desperate, and I realized that Joel was right: I needed to write some sort of showcase for myself and get myself new representation. But the minute I would resolve to do it, I would sink into sickening terror. "What would I do?" I kept asking myself. "What would I write and how?" It seemed wholly impossible.

"You're overthinking it," Joel said. "It's not like you have to write *Long Day's Journey into Night*. Take a character sketch you wrote in that weekend memoir thing and, you know, flesh it out, expand on it—whatever. Take a class, maybe."

And so I did.

The solo-show workshop I found seemed promising at first:

many of the graduates had gone on to successfully produce
their shows; one had been made into a movie. Ours was an inti-
mate group of four writers led by a slack-jawed fellow named
Hank, an amiable if somewhat dull guy who had spent most of
his life on a farm in central California. While Hank wasn't a
writer himself, he was a script consultant and had helped shape
countless scripts for some successful screenwriters, whose blurbs
of recommendation graced the workshop's pamphlets and ads.
The other writers, like me, had no real writing experience, but
after a brief interview-audition with Hank, we were accepted
on the basis of our "potential" and our willingness "to try."
One of my classmates was a woman with multiple personality
disorder who was writing a series of monologues and songs
from her various personalities' points of view. All of her personalities shared the belief that they were God, which was extremely interesting, if somewhat hard to delineate, and it seemed
to have great potential: sort of a musical version of *Sybil*, or
*The Three Faces of Eve*. There was also a feminist cowgirl from
Mexico who was writing a solo show about being raped by her
dad and maybe her brother. I say "maybe" because it was hard
to know definitively, since her writing style was lyrical, sym-
bolic, and dense, often spinning out into disturbing, invective-
laced haiku. The last member of our group was Bob. Bob sold
insurance in Toluca Lake. He was old and alcoholic and never
brought in anything to read, so I don't know what he was
working on. But he did comment, a lot, mostly hostile, offen-
sive remarks about the feminist cowgirl's stuff, which in turn
made her absolutely furious. She had a great deal of pent-up
and not-so-pent-up anger at men, so being treated to Bob's endless stream of truculent baiting made for an awfully uncomfortable four hours each week. The feminist cowgirl would read her
latest thing for about thirty-five minutes (we were supposed to

bring in fifteen minutes tops), after which Hank would limply ask some innocuous questions about "tracking" the protagonist's narrative. Then Bob, unsolicited, would wonder aloud, like a character out of *The Accused*, if rape was something that in some way the victim deep down *really wanted*; wasn't the sexual revolution meant to free us all of our inhibitions; was memory, in fact, something that could ever be truly *reliable*, etc., etc., and the feminist cowgirl would grow red-faced and start screaming at him. He would continue in his passive-aggressive way with lame little musings, she would continue to scream, and Hank, the multiple-personality-disordered chick, and I would just sit there, shuffling papers, not knowing if we should pipe in or go make some Red Zinger tea. As uncomfortable as it was, however, I didn't quit the class. It forced me to write each week, so I stayed for a few months, until I had the faint beginnings of one of the pieces that would ultimately become my solo show. One day, the feminist cowgirl called me up and said she had access to the rec room in the basement of a friend's Mar Vista apartment building and thought it would be fun to put up an evening of the stuff we had written so far in the workshop. She said that the multiple-personality-disordered chick was game (she blew Bob off), and she had one other friend who was writing a show about sleeping her way through Burning Man. I instantly agreed. The rec room was full to capacity the night of the readings, and before I was even done with my piece, I was convinced that doing a full-scale solo show was the right path. I went home that night, left Hank a voice mail message that I was quitting the workshop, started writing, and didn't stop. Six months later, I unveiled my first-ever fully developed piece of writing: a solo show called *I Slept with Jack Kerouac and Other Stories*.

Inspired in part by my second and final devastating breakup

with the Jazz Musician and his insistence that he could no longer commit because he was "the reincarnation of Jack Kerouac," the three-monologue piece costarred a talking cat and a massive, anthropomorphized penis shadow puppet, with which I shared a bittersweet pas de deux to Natalie Cole's "I've Got Love on My Mind." Joel served as producer as well as musical director (all three monologues were accompanied by incidental music).

*Kerouac* opened to a favorable review and a "recommended" from the *LA Weekly*, leading, incredibly, to coverage from other papers and magazines, including the *Los Angeles Times*. Suddenly, I started getting calls for meetings, interviews, and auditions and invitations to lunches and brunches. The enthusiasm of these suitors seemed bound to resuscitate my flatlining acting career, and, even more amazingly, there was interest in me as a writer as well.

"I knew you could do it," Joel said, hugging me, after we read the *Times* review online in the middle of the night. "See? All you had to do was put yourself out there . . ."

Hal-le-fucking-lujah!

Here was my door. Finally.

I went to a few meetings with Hollywood big shots—film executives and television producers—ostensibly to "kick around ideas" about what to "do with me" and to see if there was anything more that could come of this "little live stage thing." In brightly lit waiting rooms in office bungalows on studio lots or in mod Wilshire Boulevard agency headquarters, I sat and watched headsetted receptionists reflexively connecting calls amidst windows with panoramic views of a parched, palm-dotted haze.

"Can I get you a bottle of water?" the assistants asked.

"Sure—thank you."

"Room temp or chilled?"

It seems silly, but the assistants' questions made me anxious, as though there were a *right* answer, a more successful-person-sounding answer, an answer given by someone who actually had answers. Surmising that chilled water would be more likely to make me have to pee, I always chose room temp, though it was all for naught. I never even opened the bottles. They would sit beside me, uncracked, on coffee tables or conference tables during these meetings, and leave with me, soon to litter the floor of my tiny car. In time, the passenger side's floor would begin to resemble a water bottle graveyard, but I would never move them or throw them away. They were my little parting gifts, proof that I had been there.

The whole water bottle phenomenon seemed so strange to me. As an actor going on meetings or auditions, I was never offered something to quench my thirst. I was never offered anything at all except warnings posted on enormous angry placards that hung in the waiting areas of the various casting offices: "*ACTORS MAY NOT EAT IN THIS AREA!!!*" they screamed from above a comfy couch; "*NO ACTORS ALLOWED!!*" they hissed next to coffee machines and refrigerators; "*ACTORS: CLEAN UP YOUR GARBAGE!!*" they beseeched. I remember seeing that last one once in an office in the theater district in New York and initially misreading it as "*ACTORS ARE GARBAGE!!*" But even if those weren't the actual words, there was no mistaking the sentiment. So the proffered water bottles felt a little like keys to the city.

I was really excited about these meetings, even though I was never sure afterward what we had really talked about or what exactly the point was. The meetings were pleasant, the executives complimentary, but an unstated bewilderment hung in the air, a kind of mental "soooooo . . ." followed by seat shifting.

Sitting across from these casual, relaxed people on their over-stuffed leather furniture, I wondered how—or for that matter, when—projects got made. These people did a lot of lunch and dinner; they went to the gym and played golf; they took their wives, girlfriends, and lovers up the coast to stay in nine-hundred-dollar-a-night treehouses. I imagined them taking meetings with people like me all day, blithely discussing "high concepts," "back ends," and "protagonist arcs" until it was time to take a lunch meeting, after which they would come back and take a few more meetings until dinner.

The executives invariably came back a few times to see my show, bringing with them assistants, associates, and colleagues who sat in the audience chatting while the performance was in progress. Not accustomed, I suppose, to the mores of live theater and how to exist in an audience, they noisily discussed how to best utilize me and my material as though they were ensconced in a private pitch meeting. Because a good deal of my show was addressed directly to the audience, I could see them having these conversations for almost the entire ninety minutes. However weird that was, it was even weirder to show up in their offices afterward to hear what they had to suggest. One big shot film producer who thought my show might have potential as a film called me from his car weeping rhapsodies after he first saw it (I'm not kidding; he was *crying* in his voice mail message!). While still enthusiastic when I arrived in his office for a meeting to "suss things out," he suggested right off the bat that I should change the title, as it was too "off-putting." There were simply too many people, he insisted, who hadn't the vaguest idea who the hell Jack Kerouac was. *Really?* I was astonished and told him so.

"Well, of course, *I* know," he smiled, leaning back in his club chair. "But my *wife* hasn't a clue. She liked the show but thought you were trying to prove how smart you are by *referencing* someone as remote as Kerouac."

I must admit, I was flattered; no one had ever accused me of being too smart, so I was feeling very win-win about this. On the other hand, I didn't want to seem pompous or turn anyone off so, nodding a nod of deep concern, I consciously unfurrowed my baffled brow and widened my eyes so as to seem approachable to someone like this guy's wife.

"I mean," he continued, "you don't wanna be turning someone like my wife off. She's your audience! Know what I mean?"

I did know what he meant. A little. In an effort to build audience, Joel and I had procured the mailing list for the L.A. production of *The Vagina Monologues* and sent out postcards to the hundreds of addresses on it. The mailing resulted in a fortuitous bump in ticket sales, predominantly in the demographic of upper-middle-class women from Newport Beach. This group of women—referred to by my production crew as "the Ladies from Orange County"—would prove to be extremely loyal fans. They would trek up to L.A. once, twice, some even three times, returning with their mothers/sisters/friends, and request a post-performance photo op with me. Beautiful, blond, tan, fit—they were popular-crowd types, and their "you go, girl" fawning, sunny California smiles, and encouraging words were so heartening that I would go back to my dressing room after they left each time and cry, telling my reflection in my dressing room mirror how grateful I was, both for their kindness and for finally being in a place emotionally where I was able to receive it.

So I was troubled by the idea that the producer's wife thought I was pretentious. As far as I could tell, the Ladies from Orange County either (a) knew who Jack Kerouac was or (b) were unfazed by the mystery. But I wanted to be open; he was a very nice guy, this producer, and I was surprised and intrigued by his interest in me to begin with, and willing to see where it could lead, if anywhere.

*My Big Fat Greek Wedding* was in the movie theaters at the time and a huge hit. It too had started as a little solo show. Why not, the producer wondered aloud, make my show more like that?

"Everyone in town is looking for the next 'Fat Greek Anything,'" he told me.

My show was not even remotely similar in content or structure to *My Big Fat Greek Wedding*, especially the title piece about my breakup's aftermath, my subsequent despondency, and the ensuing visit to a well-regarded East Village witch. Upon reading my tarot cards, the witch proclaims The Jazz Musician and I soul mates and further instructs that his dumping of me is "royally fucking the order of the Universe." Her Rx is to give me a rather large, fire-engine-red candle shaped like a penis to burn, along with a spell to bring about his return (true story). Instead of the Jazz Musician, however, the magic conjures Kerouac himself into my Greenwich Village living room, who thereupon takes me on a madcap joyride to exorcise the boyfriend and teach me a life lesson in the process (dramatic license).

As I sat in the producer's office, I imagined my show as one of those transparencies teachers were always writing all over in middle school. If I draped a transparency of my show on top of one of *My Big Fat Greek Wedding* on an overhead projector, what would the image look like? I was coming up blank.

"See," the producer continued, "the *Fat Greek Wedding* is very *feel-good*, know what I mean? Your show is a bit more . . . *subversive* in some ways, especially with that giant giggling . . . *schlong* you had in the background—what was that again?"

"It was a shadow puppet of a dick candle on a scrim, lit from behind."

"*Riiight* . . . so, see, things like that are, you know—I mean, it's *great*, don't get me wrong, *very* cool, very *New Yorky*, very *arty*. But I'm just—and I'm just thinking out loud now, you know, *riffing*, so bear with me—but is there a way that you could—like they do in the *Fat Wedding*—have more stuff about *family*?"

"Family?"

"Because *family* is just money in the bank. Everyone wants to see things about family and how, you know, in the end, that's what we *are* and *who* we *are* and all that, you know?"

My family popped into my head. I saw us all together at Christmas, the one time a year when everyone got together. I saw everyone as usual barely able to contain their contempt for one another, trading obligatory gifts, insults, and hostile remarks while pill-popping downers or tossing back drink after drink to numb out. I thought about how on these visits it was impossible not to notice how interminably uncomfortable the beds in our old bedrooms were. Lumpy mattresses, hard pillows—it was as though my mother didn't want anyone to get too-too comfy, psychically short-sheeting us out of extending our visits. No sooner would our bags be placed in the foyer than she would ask, "What train are you taking back?" I thought about how my parents made my mother's grossly overweight sister "dead to them," and how they didn't speak to my mother's parents at all. I thought about the fact that my hippie uncle ran away to India and wrote us a letter saying he wasn't related to us anymore. I thought about how my eighty-year-old grandfather was almost given the boot from his assisted-living facility when he got caught getting a blow job from a brain-damaged woman half his age, incapacitated due to a massive aneurysm. I thought about how my mother, without telling me, had our two golden retrievers put to sleep so she could "redecorate the basement," and how, when I became hysterical after arriving home a month later from college to find the dogs dead, she very pointedly informed me that I was not to "ruin everyone's Thanksgiving" with my "goddamn theatrics." I thought about how no one got along or particularly liked one another, about how often they told me I sucked as a daughter/sister/aunt and how much I silently thought that they sucked right back. As all of this flashed through my mind, sitting in that office, I had to wonder, could I ever shoehorn any of this *mishegoss* into "feel-good"?

"Do you have some wacky characters in your family? Maybe throw those in the mix and focus on the boyfriend-breaking-up-with-you story and, you know, change the title to something a little more commercial? You said the boyfriend was fat, right? Maybe *My Big Fat Stupid Boyfriend?* Not *that*, but, you know, *like* that . . ."


Toward the end of the run of *Kerouac*, we produced a breast cancer benefit, which entailed a performance of my show followed by three *Playboy* Playmates reading excerpts from *On the Road* in bikinis. The day after the benefit, Miss October called me, out of breath and excited.

"My manager wants to meet you! He thinks you're great! He's really nice and cool, and he used to represent Beverly D'Angelo! I think he's interested in repping you! Here's his number. Call him right away! Good luck, Nancy!"

I thanked her and called the manager, and we set up an appointment for the next afternoon.

"I always thought Beverly D'Angelo was hot," Joel said as we wended our way over to her former manager's office for the late-afternoon appointment.

"*Vacation, Hair,*" he continued. "I could see you doing stuff like that . . ."

I don't know how we decided Joel should accompany me to this meeting or why. Looking back, it seems interesting that he was there, as if we both knew that this was something we would later be glad he was there to witness.

Aside from Miss October, I didn't know of anyone else the manager represented; his Beverly D'Angelo association had been over for almost twenty years. Still, I had high hopes; he had been getting Miss October guest spots on TV and in films, and a producer I knew spoke highly of him, saying he had connections with major talent agencies.

"You know," Beverly D'Angelo's Former Manager had told me during our brief phone conversation, "you remind me of Beverly."

Arriving at his "office"—a stucco-walled prefab condo on a nondescript, unchicly-south-of-Olympic block in West L.A.—we met Beverly D'Angelo's Former Manager. He was a grizzled guy on the north side of sixty-five, lazing about his living room in sweats and a stained undershirt, eating whitefish salad from Junior's Deli on Stoned Wheat Thins. He offered us some Clamato, which we politely declined, and then the three of us sat down for the meeting on a scruffy pleather playpen sofa strewn with head shots, copies of *Playboy*, and dusty videotapes. Throughout the ensuing conversation, Beverly D'Angelo's Former Manager would continue to partake of the whitefish salad–cracker combo, whitefish dribbling off here and there, further imbruing his already soiled top and spackling the deep folds around his mouth.

"Thanks for coming," he said, cheeks full and vibrating, taking the head shot and résumé I handed him. There was some uncomfortable silence, but not so uncomfortable that it was unknown to me; this was the space that I had waited out hundreds of times before as someone got to know me via a single page of typed credits wherein the gaps between gigs were presented in that seamless way that insisted it was all intentional. Beverly D'Angelo's Former Manager chewed and read and read and chewed, all the while breathing through his nose, which made a faint whistling sound, like a faraway train on a dreamy trip, destination unknown. A few moments and a sip of Clamato later, Beverly D'Angelo's Former Manager finally spoke.

"So. I saw your show, and I was very, very impressed. You are, without question, extremely talented."

"Thank you," I said, pleased. "Thank you very much."

He paused for a second, considering me. Then, looking back down at my head shot, he regarded it for another moment before flipping it over to once again peruse my résumé. A few more seconds and then:

"You're talented, you're pretty, and you're funny," he pronounced finally. "So, I have just one question for you."

"All right."

"Why haven't you made it?"

"What do you mean?"

"I mean just what I asked: *Why haven't you made it? Why aren't you successful?*"

Time stopped; the question hung in the air. He continued.

"I saw your show, I'm looking at you now, and I'm baffled. You had all the ingredients. But now—I look at this résumé, filled with junk, old credits, nothing that anyone gives a shit about, and I have to ask: *WHY?*"

Beverly D'Angelo's Former Manager leaned in to me, as if imploring me to untangle it all for him.

"Why aren't you more successful?" he entreated before adding piteously, "What happened to you?"

At first, not knowing what to say, I didn't answer. Beverly D'Angelo's Former Manager continued with the blandishments about how I really could have "done it," and after the initial stunned silence, a lame attempt at a reply tumbled across my lips, after which I found myself suddenly floating, looking down at the three of us from the vantage point of the broken track lights above. Joel and Beverly D'Angelo's Former Manager continued to talk, positing theories, speaking in generalities, concluding nothing. The meeting thus ended, the same way most meetings had, with vague plans about "keeping in touch" and the promise of future meetings that we all knew, deep down, would never be scheduled.

Several weeks later, my show closed. Beverly D'Angelo's Whitefish-Encrusted Former Manager never called; the south-of-Olympic-condo episode became yet another appalling show-biz tale I'd tell over multiple glasses of over-oaked chardonnay. I would relish relating the story, as usual, painting myself as the unwitting victim of the unspeakable terrorism waged by Shit-Heel Hollywood Men, hell-bent on pissing on my parade.

"If only you'd had the presence of mind to say x, y, and z . . ." friends would supportively cluck, shaking their heads in bemused amazement at yet another one of my messes. Publicly, I would milk the story for laughs; privately, I hid behind my outrage, numbing myself with booze, Xanax, cigarettes, repudiation—whatever was around—until I felt nothing at all. But then a funny thing happened. I started to see Beverly D'Angelo's Former Manager everywhere: in my head when I was running on the treadmill, in the mirror when I was brushing my teeth, in my dreams.

*Why aren't you successful? What happened?*

It wasn't that he was taunting me; he was just insisting that I not dismiss him, looking expectantly at me to continue the conversation I had hastily abandoned. But this time, there would be no escape—Beverly D'Angelo's Former Manager refused to let me go.

For a while, it was easy to hide behind my indignation. "Such an asshole," I would say to myself. How dare he?" Insulted, ego wounded, I tried to dismiss the affront as nothing more than the bitter ramblings of a has-been flesh peddler, a slob whose claim to fame was that a million years ago he represented someone famous. But there was a small part of me—very small—that recognized that this was one of those moments in life when something or someone appears out of the ether, Yoda-like, to confront you with that which you fear most. There, in that stuffy condo on the wrong side of Olympic, far from home, far from myself, I was face-to-face with the question I had been avoiding for as long as I could remember.

*Why aren't you successful?*

Beyond the tawdriness and the shirt stains and the stench of subpar deli fish spreads, there was something to be gleaned from this low-rent Buddha. Perhaps his question was not to be taken literally or as an insult, but more as a riddle or koan: not answerable rationally per se, but understood on an intuitive level to inspire a process of further questioning. In my defensive fluster, I never once considered the actual *question*; I was far too caught up in the *answer* I thought he expected. There may not have been any one specific answer, but what did I understand of the question at all? Beverly D'Angelo's Former Manager may have thought I was a failure, but what did *I* think? What did *I* think of success? Did it mean fame? Did it mean making tons of money? Did it mean respect as an artist in a world I longed to be included in? Did it mean being happy? How much of what happened or didn't happen with my career was within my control? Did I want it—to be a successful actor? I thought I did. But if so, to what extent? Allowing the question to subdivide, I was able to, as the Zen masters say, "shock my mind into awareness," but still I couldn't quite know then what it meant, only that it meant more than I was able to, at that moment, see. The Beverly D'Angelo's Former Manager sightings continued sporadically, and then one day, instead of running or tuning out or looking the other way, I decided to simply stare him down. He didn't really have any power; he was only a ghost. And then I remembered that while most ghosts come to haunt seeking retribution or, perhaps, rectification, some have had their sleep interrupted by the excessive grief of the living. Beverly D'Angelo's Former Manager didn't deserve an answer to the queries he posed sitting on that *farkakte* couch. I, however, did.

## 13.  The Girl in the Peacoat

**During my last** year or so in Los Angeles, I discovered, like the characters in *The Day of the Locust*, that "the sunshine wasn't enough." Life wasn't lived, just halfheartedly tolerated, day in, day out, the same complacent languor masquerading as equanimity until five or so, when we'd all drink lots of wine, get hammered, have dinner, and go to bed. *Kerouac* was over; despite all the promising reviews, the meetings, *the buzz* . . . I had nothing to show for it except a handful of clippings.

One of the associations it did yield, however, was with a television producer–slash–writer's manager from a major management company who wooed me into writing something to which he could be attached as a producer. We had many meetings at his office overlooking the verdant courtyard's cascading fountain, which was full of flower petals and the tossed pennies of writers hoping to become the next Alan Ball. I agreed to take a crack at writing an original spec pilot. I figured, hey, this guy has connections; it might help open some doors for me acting-wise. All I need, I kept thinking to myself, was one good thing to happen—that's all I need. So, even though I'd never written a teleplay before, I decided to give it a whirl. And what a whirl it was: I was miserable and uninspired, and dreaded facing it each day. My heart would race every time I sat down to work, so I would write a line of dialogue then reward myself with a cigarette and a Klonopin. I'd write a bit more; then pour myself a glass of wine. Then another and another, then have another smoke; then I'd take a nap. When I would wake, I would make some black coffee and start all over again. This went on almost every day for two months. I was turning into Carson McCullers. In the midst of all this, I flew east to meet with a director interested in working on a New York production of *Kerouac*, who suggested that if I did a rewrite, we could mount it at one of the venerable downtown theaters with which he was associated. I readily agreed, taking his notes with me back to California. Then I heard from an off-Broadway producer who had produced the solo shows of some amazing performers whose work I idolized. He, too, was interested in my show, and he was hooked into those same downtown theaters.

Shortly thereafter, I turned in an appallingly bad pilot script, got notes telling me that it was appallingly bad, and felt no interest in revising it. *The script had issues*, the producer said, it *needed to be reworked*, blah-blah-blah . . . I just didn't care anymore. I don't know what about all this made me snap, but it did. I was done. The arrows were pointing me toward New York. Though I had initially thought I would go back and forth when the time came to do a production of my show, after consideration, Joel and I decided instead to leave L.A. and try living in New York, at least for a while. As much as it made sense, it felt so weird and sudden. "Wait—I love living in California!" I thought to myself. "Don't I?" *Do I?*

How many times during those eight years did I think to myself, Dorothy-like, "I wanna go home," and wish that all I needed was just a pair of bitchin' shoes? Nevertheless, when the time came to actually leave L.A., I was consumed by a tremendous sadness. Our last day in town, I wrote a free-association list of things that made me think of L.A. on a scrap of paper to keep in my wallet:

Coyotes, car exhaust, Apple Pan, In-N-Out, Chateau Marmont (for drinks), Chateau Marmutt (for dogs), Santa Anas, bergamot, Coffee Bean, Burton Way, helicopters, Beachwood Canyon, Erewhon, Chalet Gourmet, Pink's, Ralph's, Hal's, Joe's, Lola's, Art deco, dead palm kernels . . .

My parents greeted the news of our leaving L.A. with a shock and disappointment I had both dreaded and anticipated. I had known that they wouldn't view our move to New York— despite its proximity to them in Connecticut—as a positive thing, that they would see it as throwing in the towel, even with my confidence that a New York staging of my show was imminent.

"What about your agent?" my father asked when I initially called to inform them. "How can you leave *him*?"

"Yes," my mother said, joining in on the other extension. "You seem to be making some headway—finally! Changing directions midstream seems like not the best idea, if you ask me . . ."

"What agent? I don't have an agent," I told them quietly. "That's . . . that's kind of the whole problem."

There was a pause; the sound of a sitcom's canned laughter crested in the background. When you're disillusioned with yourself, can there be anything more unbearable than the weight of other people's chagrin?

"What about your house?" my father continued. "And the *weh-thuh*? You gonna leave *awl* that nice *weh-thuh* to go back to that shithole city?"

He didn't wait for my answer; he just hung up, and I was left listening to my mother breathing and the forced gaiety of a television show on which I would never appear.

Joel and I decided to drive across the country instead of fly-ing; I told myself that this was because we had a dog and two cats, but I had another reason for wanting to leave Los Angeles by car: I couldn't bear the idea of getting on a plane and exit-ing in a flash. I needed to pull away carefully so that the vistas I'd come to know so well could recede slowly, just another drive on just another day. It was, as usual, a lovely, temperate after-noon: sunny, seventy-five degrees, "unhealthy for sensitive groups" air quality. I took one last look toward the mountains before climbing into the car, remembering how my first room-mate, Jeff, had told me to look for them when I drove in all those years before. Face the mountains and you are looking north; take a left and you're at the beach. If you can keep those things straight, he'd said, you will never lose your way. Funny how you can know where you're going but end up lost all the same.

It was autumn when we arrived in New York, the day before my thirty-seventh birthday. The light had changed over from summer, and the air had just the faintest whisper of crispness. Walking around those first few days back in the city, I kept thinking of a charcoal gray J.Crew peacoat I once had that would have been the perfect weight for the season. The coat had been a gift from my mother for Christmas the year after the Jazz Musician and I split. I couldn't remember the last time I'd seen it, let alone worn it, but it was gone forever, that I was cer-tain of. A few years prior, my brother and his then girlfriend—another actor—had undertaken a redecorating project of the apartment that was my former home. In the midst of this, some-one had tossed the ill-fated peacoat, along with several other ar-ticles of clothing and a smallish box full of pictures and other mementos. In fairness, I hadn't been too terribly aggressive in pursuing those belongings and ensuring their safe return; I seem to recall we spoke, the girlfriend and I, on the phone about the issue of my "crap," but whether it was clear that I didn't want the stuff thrown away, I don't know. Thinking of that peacoat aroused thoughts of other possessions I had tucked to the far right and back of a small closet in my former digs: a long, rayon, bias-cut print dress from the forties, found in a thrift store in Vermont in the eighties; a black spandex catsuit and two very sexy jackets from Charivari, gifts from the Jazz Musician when we first met. The small box had had some marked-up scripts and notebooks, a few bootleg jazz cassette tapes, but mostly it had contained photographs of my life from NYU up to the time I left for L.A.: in costume as the Psycho Ex-Girlfriend from Hell on *Remote Control*; in the decadently formfitting aubergine Edwardian dress as Madame in *The Maids*; in the fat suit as the *Funnyhouse of a Negro* landlady; as Helen of Troy, wearing something tattered and vaguely Grecian, straddling my Paris. There had been some production stills from the *After School Special*; photos of me holding Jane's birthday cake while she blew out her candles; photos of the Jazz Musician, us lying on a bed together, somewhere in the Pacific Northwest, laughing.

What had made me so cavalier about that stuff? Even after my brother had taken over the apartment with the proviso that I could come collect my things later, why would I have left them to the whims of others when the responsibility for those effects was really mine? I'd had enough therapy by that time to suspect that in some ways the doomed fate of those relics was fully intentional, that I'd kept them out of sight, far from review, for a reason. Perhaps seeing fragments of the person I had been before the last eight years in L.A. would only attest to how beaten down, how fruitless I felt, after all. Unencumbered by these remainders, maybe I could be more flexible in how I viewed myself and where I had come to since being the girl I had so long ago stuffed into a box and left behind. Conflicted though I was—about both the girl and her memories—I couldn't help feeling sad to have lost them both.

In time, L.A. faded into the distance, and in the year that followed, I finished the revised script, got a theatrical agent, and cocreated a reading series called *Cause Celeb!*, which would ultimately go on to have a four-year run. The theater director with whom I was going to work on *Kerouac* ended up having far too difficult a schedule to plan around, so the off-Broadway producer set up meeting after meeting with other directors, as well as designers and dramaturges, all of whom had opinions. There were visits to theaters and communications with theater companies; there were conversations with general managers and other producers about additional financing. I would emerge from these meetings thinking they had the same level of pointlessness as the ones in Hollywood.

Eighteen months after we arrived back in New York, I discovered that I was pregnant. It was agreed that the show would be put off until after the baby came; there was talk about a production in late spring, the following fall—something. But as the baby grew inside me, so too did the nagging suspicion that the *Kerouac* show would never see production. The off-Broadway producer could never fully commit; each encounter with him was accompanied by the slightest whiff of bullshit. But even that wasn't why I knew for almost certain that I would never perform my show again. All of a sudden, it seemed like a past moment: something done, finished, and not worth revisiting. Strangely, I didn't feel like doing it anymore, even as a way of getting attention as an actor.

There were other revelations: at first, I thought of the pregnancy as a little detour in my career progress; everything had to be put on hold until I could get my body "back." But in fact, I had it backward. For years, the only thing that had really been on hold was me. Getting pregnant gave me time to focus, time to reflect. I grew bigger and bigger, and as I did, I would take off my clothes and stand naked in front of the mirror, studying my tits, my ass, my roundness, from every angle, awed by the magnificence of my soon-to-be-thirty-five-pounds-heavier self. "Pregnancy," I would marvel. "Preg-NANCY." Making a whole person inside gave me an unqualified opportunity to consider the whole person outside. I was finally *exercising my will*, in my own life; there was nothing stalled or ambiguous about it, and even if I didn't have all the answers, I knew one thing for damn sure: I never wanted to hate myself again.

We moved a few months into my pregnancy; the one-room furnished loft we had been renting wasn't baby-friendly. I needed a place with walls, even if it was only one. We found a place, got our stuff out of storage, and began to slowly unpack. One day, I was pulling things out of a box when I came across a black-and-white photograph in a Plexiglas frame, taken in the winter of 1994 by the fashion photographer Bill Cunningham. It was from his Sunday *New York Times* On the Street column, a picture of me, wearing the lost peacoat. I had no idea my photo had been snapped that day in 1994—right around the time I was meeting with Lorne Michaels and rehearsing *Troilus and Cressida*—and happened upon it only by chance as I sat in bed with my coffee and cat. I remember looking at his column that day (a study in the sudden inclination toward peacoats!) and seeing a girl whom I initially thought looked pretty cool, until, of course, I realized, holy shit—it's . . . *me*. Once I had that figured out, I seized the moment as yet another occasion to pick my looks apart, wishing I was thinner, chicer, prettier . . . whatever. I didn't even pause for a second to feel good about being one of Cunningham's subjects in the first place, nor did I keep my copy of the paper. It was only later that evening that I frantically called my mother, who had, thankfully, already found it, torn it out, and stuffed it into the Plexiglas frame from CVS.

"There she is," I thought, standing there almost eleven years later: the girl I had left in the box, in black and white, captured by a stranger. Perhaps not the most flattering photo, but it was "the truth of the moment," as Mamet would say: wholly accurate, depicting a young woman confidently striding along a city street, arms swinging, jaunty, sauntering, a bit insouciant. She is wearing all black (except for the peacoat), all baggy, and of course, her long dark hair and bangs mostly obscure her face. She is, after all, "the girl with the hair in her face." To the casual eye, she looks self-possessed and confident. But there is something off and perhaps deceptive about her assertive glide. While her gait advances her forward with seeming gusto, her torso leans back and away, suggesting reluctance, circumspection. And yet her gaze to the left, even covered with all that messy hair, suggests expectancy, eagerness, and all kinds of fun. But here's the part I missed all those years before, when I was so hasty to sleuth out flaws: she may have been a bit too angry, too quick to say "fuck you," too easy (or too difficult) to get into bed, or too vacillating about what she wanted or thought she wanted, what with all her big ideas about art, but her enthusiasm, her devotion, her willingness to try—these were there too. She was afraid—deeply—and yet, *she did it anyway*. And, despite all her misgivings, life propelled her forward, even as she hung back. Looking at her, I decided that I still thought she was cool, only this time without qualification. And more important, I realized that the girl in the picture wasn't lost at all. She was there all the time, only now sharing space with the other girl, the one I was carrying inside me.

I never formally declared I was giving up acting—maybe because I haven't. Anyway, I don't think many actors actually do. You may go on to do other things, you may never act again and still, you don't say it. Perhaps it's too painful, even years later, to utter the words "I gave up acting" or "I'm not an actor anymore." Or maybe it's because you hold out just a tiny bit of, not hope . . . let's say fantasy that something, some part, in the right circumstances might coax you back to stand once again in someone else's clothes, speak someone else's words, under the lights. Or maybe it's just not something you can shed: once you're an actor, you're an actor for life. By the way, I still think I would make a pretty fucking fabulous Alexandra Del Lago, aka "the Princess Kosmonopolis," in *Sweet Bird of Youth*. And I'm the perfect age—"not old," as the Princess would say, "just not young." The age when you know for sure that there is no victory over time—the trick is to be heard. Because, remember folks, only people who are full of shit whisper.

# Acknowledgments

I am eternally grateful to the following people and animals:

My agent and *knight-errant*, the brilliant (and ridiculously hot) Bill Clegg.

My superb, exceptionally insightful editor, Anton Mueller, who descended in a Glinda-like bubble of serendipity.

Panio Gianopoulos for his edits and notes on the first draft.

Colin Dickerman for his friendship, his guidance, and for buying my book in the first place.

Matt Hudson.

Rachel Mannheimer.

Everyone at Bloomsbury USA.

Joe Danisi and Stephanie Cannon—the awesomely fabulous directors of Naked Angels Tuesdays@9, where many of these pages were first read.

Two phenomenal writers who are equally phenomenal friends, Mike Albo and Cintra Wilson—I am forever in your debt and love you both so much!

Robin Aiello, Tom Bollinger, Baret Boisson, Edward Burke, Ken Burrows, Charles Busch, Meg Busch, Joan Byfield, Rob d'Entremont, Scott Durkin, Hope Edelman, Florence Falk, Peter Frechette, the Goodman family, Barbara Graham, Daintry Jensen, Hettie Jones, Wendy, Gerry, and Kimberly Kleinbaum,

Cintia Marangoni, Dave Menendez, Eric Myers, Michelle Phillips, Michelle Rivera, Tisha "Teddy" Slote, Daleet Spector, Toby Tumarkin, Joanna Virello, Vivien, Jacob, and Uri Zighelboim, the members of the ASH-X salon, all the guys down at Pasita, and of course my parents, for their many years of support.

A huge Kathleen Turner–style bow to the audiences of *I Slept With Jack Kerouac and Other Stories* (especially the Ladies from Orange County); *Cause Celeb!*, *Schwag*, and, last but not least, Naked Angels Tuesdays@9 (*especially* the actors—I love you guys!!).

Ira and Fosse—I love you; thank you for loving me.

Max—I miss you.

My husband, best friend, and first editor, Joel, for endlessly championing my dreams, and even though you once told me I should "leave things like leaf descriptions to people like William Faulkner," I love you with all my heart.

My darling, Colette, who makes every day beautiful . . . I love you, sweet girl, so, SO much! Hurray, Boo Boo Bear!! Let's go get our sundaes!!

And finally, I would like to thank David Mamet, without whose long-ago encouragement and inspiration there would be no book.

## A Note on the Author

Nancy Balbirer is the author and star of the critically acclaimed solo show *I Slept With Jack Kerouac and Other Stories* and the cocreator of the cult reading series *Cause Celeb!* She has costarred on *Seinfeld* and MTV's *Remote Control*, performed off-Broadway, and appears regularly in New York City's alternative cabaret scene. She is a graduate of NYU's Tisch School of the Arts and the co-owner, designer, and doyenne of the West Village boîte Pasita. She lives in Manhattan with her husband and daughter.